Too Smart

Too Smart

How Digital Capitalism Is Extracting Data, Controlling Our
Lives, and Taking Over the World

Jathan Sadowski

The MIT Press
Cambridge, Massachusetts
London, England

This book was set in Stone Serif and Stone Sans by Jen Jackowitz. Printed and bound in the United States of America.

Library of Congress Cataloging-in-Publication Data

Names: Sadowski, Jathan, author.
Title: Too smart : how digital capitalism is extracting data, controlling
    our lives, and taking over the world / Jathan Sadowski.
Description: Cambridge, Massachusetts : MIT Press, [2020] | Includes
    bibliographical references and index.
Identifiers: LCCN 2019025848 | ISBN 9780262538589 (paperback)
Subjects: LCSH: Technological innovations--Social aspects. |
    Technological innovations--Economic aspects.
Classification: LCC HM846 .S23 2020 | DDC 303.48/3--dc23
LC record available at https://lccn.loc.gov/2019025848

10 9 8 7 6 5 4 3 2 1

Contents

Acknowledgments

This book is the product of a large network of people who contributed in important ways—intellectually, socially, and professionally—to the work that went into making it a real thing. There's no way I could do justice to the exhaustive list of people who deserve to be acknowledged, so broad strokes will have to do.

Thanks go to my family, who have provided constant support and encouragement, even when they weren't totally sure what I was doing, first as a grad student studying across the country and then as an academic working around the world. But they knew it was something I cared a lot about, and they helped me pursue opportunities in any way they could.

Thanks go to my friends in all the places I have lived and traveled who have kept me sane while I researched the ideas in this book. I can't name you all—the Tempe crew, the Delft crew, the Sydney crew, the placeless crew whom I see wherever and whenever I can—but you know who you are.

Not to play favorites, but I would be remiss if I didn't recognize the two people I talk to almost every day. Sophia Maalsen is the best work wife anybody could ever hope for. Our daily chats and coffee walks provide the kind of relationship and routine that is necessary for a good life. Amy Graff has been one of my closest friends since the moment we met. I'm grateful we have a rare kind of friendship that remains strong and active even across vast distances of space-time.

I was lucky enough to make writing this book my job. The universities where I have worked—Arizona State University, Delft University of Technology, and, particularly, the University of Sydney—have supplied me with time to do research as well as cadres of amazing colleagues to collaborate with. The different research groups and project teams I am lucky to be part of have, in their own ways, provided much needed spaces for sharing ideas, discussing ongoing work, celebrating successes, and commiserating about setbacks.

Finally, I benefit greatly from having an extended, growing network of colleagues and comrades. I have formed this community during the many days and nights spent at conferences, workshops, and symposiums, where I get to hang out with the most brilliant and generous scholars. This community has also grown through the folks I've met, conversations I've had, and lurking I've done on Twitter, which have shaped me in important ways—for better and worse. Sometimes these two places overlap, which is always both weird and fantastic. On the good days, I'm super grateful to be part of this lively community. On the bad days, I log off.

Prologue 2021: A Smart Odyssey

The world until yesterday was a dumb place. Nothing spoke, nothing listened, nothing saw, nothing knew, nothing did much of anything at all. Only the people were intelligent and animate; the things were inactive and disconnected. But then, as if they were struck by the bolt of lightning that animated Frankenstein's monster, things began to stir and switch on. It wasn't just one thing that woke up, though. Everything was energized by digital information and computation. Through sensors things can now observe, through networks they can now communicate, through algorithms and automation they can now act. Even mundane objects are more active and aware than the most complex machines of the past. The world was dumb, but now it is smart.

1 How to Think about Technology

> You talk as if a god had made the Machine. I believe that you pray to it when you are unhappy. Men made it, do not forget that. . . . The Machine is much, but it is not everything.
>
> —E. M. Forster, "The Machine Stops," 1928

You can easily trade all your dumb stuff for smart things. *Smart* is now becoming the new normal. You don't even have to seek it out. Wait long enough and the upgrades will come to you—in your home, your work, your city—if they haven't already.

Smart umbrellas light up to alert you that rain is in the forecast. Smart vehicles take over the drudgery of driving during rush hour. Smart, virtual assistants obey your every command, learn your preferences and routines, and automatically adjust accordingly. Think of a thing—whether it is a comb or city—and there is almost certainly a smart version of it available, if not multiple versions to choose from. It's not always clear why things are made smart, but that hasn't stopped the spread of smartness through society. Often it seems silly and unnecessary, if not annoying or creepy. But no thing, no space, is safe from smartification.

Besides signaling "high tech" or "new and improved," what does it actually mean for something to be smart? The label is now applied haphazardly, so definitions are not always clear and consistent. But a good, simple definition, which works well for our purposes, is that "smart" means a thing is embedded with digital technology for data collection, network connectivity, and enhanced control. Take, for instance, a smart toothbrush, which uses sensors to record when, how long, and how well you brush your teeth. Since it is Bluetooth enabled and software embedded, the smart toothbrush sends that brushing data to cloud servers owned by the manufacturer or a third party. You and your dentist can then access the data via an app, which provides "the user with real time brushing guidance and performance monitoring" that scores your daily dental hygiene, as one smart toothbrush on the market proclaims.[1] Depending on your dental insurance plan, your hygiene scores could also directly impact your monthly premiums. Good brushers get discounts, while bad brushers are punished. An honest tagline might read, "With a smart toothbrush, we know what happens in your mouth!"

These "enchanted objects," as an entrepreneur with the MIT Media Lab calls them, "will respond to our needs, come to know us, and even learn to think ahead on our behalf."[2] While the wonders of smart tech might feel like magical enchantments that enable us to cast digital spells, this book intends to dispel any notions that we inhabit the charmed castle of Fantasia. If anything, it's more like the witchy world of Sabrina, where every spell comes at a cost and unintended consequences abound.

This mystical language of enchantment echoes a famous adage by the sci-fi author Arthur C. Clarke: "Any sufficiently advanced technology is indistinguishable from magic."[3] The implication here is that the majority of people who don't have specialized technical knowledge are like the sorcerer's apprentice: they don't understand how the tech works, they are unaware of its repercussions, and they are unable to control its power.

The modest conveniences provided by smart tech are what we get in exchange for not asking too many questions about why our lives are now filled with data-collecting, internet-connected machines. Why is everything getting smart now? What else is going on behind the scenes? Who is really benefiting? The occasional scandal—when a company is caught creepily tracking people or its databases are hacked—is enough to focus our collective scorn on a specific issue, but it's usually not enough to spur deeper critical inquiry. The disgraced company will issue a mea culpa and all is forgiven—if not explicitly, then effectively when we forget about the trespass or just get used to offending events. And it's back to business as usual. We are expected to continue buying, using, and upgrading according to schedule.

Smart tech is sold as the inevitable next generation of technology. You may choose not to proactively upgrade, but eventually that choice will be made for you. Whereas smart used to be the premium option, it's now becoming the standard as things are integrated with sensors, computers, and Wi-Fi connections by default. This is more than just the "feature creep" we now expect with new gadgets, wherein more buttons and settings are crammed into the same appliance. The rapid rise of smart tech is not just the result of consumers demanding smarter things, smarter homes, and smarter cities. Rather, as this book shows, the interests of corporations and governments hold vastly more influence than consumer choice over how/why certain technologies are made and used.

Making things smart is big business: projections for the market value of the smart city sector alone—not including homes, offices, and consumer goods—hover around $1 trillion by 2020. While some market research firms are bullish—Frost & Sullivan projects the smart city's value at $1.56 trillion—even the conservative forecasts tend to be north of $500 billion.[4] The research firm Gartner predicts that the number of "connected things" in use worldwide will continue to grow exponentially, from 8.3 billion in 2017 to 20.4 billion in 2020.[5]

Media coverage of smart tech tends to be trapped between breathless excitement about cool gadgets and vague concerns about privacy and cybersecurity. To be sure, smart tech can be pretty awesome and privacy issues are important. But the impacts of smart tech are much too significant and comprehensive to warrant such clichéd takes.

A passive, shallow stance toward smart tech and its creators is a grave mistake. Smart tech is shaping up to be more than just a trend. It has become a pervasive, powerful presence in our lives and society. Thus it is marked as a technological paradigm in urgent need of critical analysis. We would be remiss to treat it as anything less.

Interests, Imperatives, Impacts

This book is not concerned with technology in the way that tech blogs review the pros and cons of a gadget, or thought leaders provide advice and predictions. Rather, it's focused more on the people, values, and organizations that are behind technology and its impacts. In other words, it is a book about politics, power, and profit—and the way they are channeled through, and changed by, technology. For short, we can call this *technopolitics*.

It's important to understand that each phase of the technical process—from design to use—is loaded with politics, and even born of politics. This book might be read as a call to politicize technology. But that would mean technology was removed from political concerns and consequences. That's not right. Instead, this book is a call to recognize the politics that have been, and continue to be, an integral part of technology all along. We should analyze the technopolitics of our emerging smart society by looking at three aspects: *interests, imperatives,* and *impacts*.

In short, the book argues for three broad technopolitical points, and shows how they manifest in various different ways and places across society:

- Smart tech advances the interests of corporate technocratic power, and over other values like human autonomy, social goods, and democratic rights.
- Smart tech is driven by the dual imperatives of digital capitalism: extracting data from, and expanding control over, potentially everything and everybody.
- Smart tech's impacts are a Faustian bargain of convenience and connection, in the Zuckerbergian sense, in exchange for a wide range of (un)intended and (un)known consequences.[6]

Whose Interests?

Technology is a way of materializing interests. Far from being objective or neutral, technology is embedded with values and intentions. Technology is, after all, the result of decisions and actions made by humans, and it is then used by humans with motivations and goals. As decades of careful study by social scientists, historians, and engineers has shown, no technology's existence is inevitable and all technologies are shaped by social processes.[7] Behind every technology is a bunch of human choices about what problems should be solved, how resources should be spent, why people should use this thing, where trade-offs should be made, and many other choices that boil down to doing X instead of Y or Z. Even when there are good reasons for making those decisions, they are still based on certain motivations, principles, values, goals, and so on.

Politics come into play when we start asking questions such as, Whose interests are represented, who's included, who benefits? And the flip side: Whose interests are erased, who's excluded, who loses? When some people's values are included, some people's voices aren't heard, and some people win while others do not, then that is the essence of politics. It's not a question of if technology is political but rather what are the politics?

Langdon Winner, a noted theorist of technopolitics, argued that "technology is itself a political phenomenon." This does not only mean that technology is a thing in need of legislation that regulates its production, features, and uses. It means, Winner contends, that technology is itself akin to a form of *legislation* because of the way "technical forms do, to a large extent, shape the basic pattern and content of human activity in our time."[8] Whether it means crafting policy or building technology, what could be more political than some people having the power to make decisions about how other people live in the world?

Legal systems are sets of rules for what is allowed, frameworks for what rights people have, and plans for what kind of society we will live in. Technical systems do the same things in different ways. They are sets of rules for what is (not) allowed, frameworks for what rights people (don't) have, and plans for what kind of society we will (not) live in. Technologies are like legislation: there's a lot of them, they don't all do the same thing, and some are more significant, but together as a system they form the foundation of society.

This theory of technopolitics is perfectly suited for analyzing the digital platforms and algorithms that mediate increasingly more of our social interactions and economic exchanges. Following from Winner, legal scholar Lawrence Lessig famously proclaimed that "code is law."[9] But this comparison almost doesn't go far enough. In response, media theorist Wendy Chun has pointed out that computer "code is better than law" because of its unwavering adherence to the rules and commands of its programmers.[10] Even the most authoritarian dictator would be unable to enforce the exact letter of the law as strictly and consistently as a computer can execute its code.

Just as with law, technologies are harnessed by elite groups to advance their own positions in and visions of the world.[11] If technology is anything like a form of legislation, then we must scrutinize those who are the legislators. They are not merely engineers crafting better machines, innovators testing new designs, or entrepreneurs taking bold risks. They are technocrats creating systems that shape society and govern people.[12] By neglecting the politics of smart tech, we allow powerful interests to reside in the shadows and exercise undue influence over our lives.

Backed by empirical research, there is consensus among political scientists that the United States is now far more of an oligarchy than a democracy.[13] The general public has little influence over which policies are put into law, while the preferences of the wealthy elite are almost always supported by policy. Not only can this same inequality in politics be seen in many other countries, I argue here that the oligarchy in making policy mirrors the oligarchy in creating technology. The design and development of technology is lorded over by the few, while the rest of the world must live with those decisions.

When citizens are disenfranchised from influencing political processes, when they are shut out from meaningful channels of input and recourse, we rightly call such a regime authoritarian.

Democracy is founded on rights to transparency about and influence over how legislation is made. We elect and lobby the legislators. We hold them accountable and threaten their positions. We contest and organize against decisions that run counter to our values and principles. Of course, these processes are not perfect. But at least we recognize the power and importance of legislation as a force in society. We recognize the necessity of being able to understand, protest, and change this force. We critique and challenge the political system. We are righteously outraged when those rights are suppressed.

Why, then, should we be willing to tolerate the fact that the technopolitical systems that shape society and impact our lives are largely created by an elite cadre of—mostly white, mostly male, extremely wealthy—corporate executives, engineers, and investors. The issues of whose interests are included in (and excluded from) technology generally and smart tech particularly is a critical concern of our time. With technopolitics as with legislative politics, when we ask, "Who really rules?" the answer is, for now, a small group of the rich and powerful.

Importantly, however, this technopolitical dynamic does not mean there is some grand conspiracy at play. The existence of oligarchic power is not evidence of a New World Order. Nor does it mean the engineers and executives necessarily have malicious intentions to harm others. What it means is that the structures of politics and technology are set up so that most people are excluded from participating in a significant way. As Winner explains, usually "it is neither correct nor insightful to say, 'Someone intended to do somebody else harm.' Rather, one must say that the technological deck has been stacked long in advance to favor certain social interests, and that some people were bound to receive a better hand than others."[14] If anything, the absence of collusion and malice makes the biased, unequal consequences of technology even more insidious.

What Imperatives?

Two major imperatives drive the design, development, and use of smart tech: collection and control. Whereas *interests* are about whose values and voices are included, *imperatives* are about the overarching principles and goals that have deeper influence and wider reach. For example, the profit motive is an imperative of capitalism, which pushes firms to maximize profits, usually as the primary or only imperative. Similarly, the imperatives I will focus on throughout the book are core parts of digital capitalism. Understanding these imperatives, and how they are manifested through smart tech will reveal much about how technopolitics operates in society.

I won't spend much time right now explaining the imperatives of collection and control because each one gets its own chapter, but I'll summarize them here. The imperative of collection is about extracting all data, from all sources, by any means possible. It compels businesses and governments to collect as much data as they can, wherever they can. Just as we expect corporations to be profit driven, we should now expect them to be data driven. This is why so much of smart tech is built to suck up data. For many industries, data is a new form of capital, and thus they are always seeking and exploiting new ways to accumulate data.

The imperative of control is about creating systems that monitor, manage, and manipulate the world and people. It's represented by the tireless surveillance systems that help corporations and police govern people, regulate access, and modify behaviors. This imperative leads to sensors embedded everywhere, everything connected to the internet, and the reliance on automation to oversee it all. Smart tech is built to expand and enhance powers of control, whether that's remote control over objects via software applications or social control over populations via algorithmic analysis. The key concern is not with control itself but rather with who has control over whom.

The imperatives of collection and control are deeply interdependent. Harvesting data requires the technical ability and social authority to probe things, people, and places. Control systems are fueled by data, which allows for more granular, more effective, and more instantaneous command over those same things, people, and places. Smart tech is the offspring of both imperatives. Many of the distinctions drawn in this book—such as explaining each imperative with its own chapter—are only meant to be analytic in nature. The distinctions give us a better idea of not only how smart tech works but also why it works the way it does, and how these imperatives are realized. Since collection and control overlap in real life, so too will they overlap in the following chapters. We can (and will) see this overlap in a myriad of examples.

It's hard to underestimate the influence these imperatives have over the design and use of smart tech. They show up in a wide range of applications, spaces, and scales. This ranges from robot vacuums secretly mapping users' homes so their manufacturers can then sell these "rich maps" to other companies, to insurers monitoring how people drive, exercise, and eat so that they can reward some behaviors and punish others.[15] As imperatives, collection and control are not new. We live under capitalism, and these imperatives have been integral parts of capitalism from the beginning. An entire library could be filled with studies about how capitalism continuously innovates new ways to extract profit and exercise power over everything—society and nature, human and nonhuman, mind and body.

My aim here is to show how these dual imperatives operate in the age of digital capitalism and smart tech. We can then understand how, why, and for whom smart tech is designed. We can identify the trends and themes that influence technological development. We can make informed predictions about what to expect in the near future—if we continue down the same path.

How Are We Impacted?

Smart tech has gone viral—spreading, infecting, reproducing, disrupting, and thriving in nearly all spaces of society and parts of our lives. David Golumbia and Chris Gilliard, scholars of technology and culture, wrote an article in early 2018 that rounded up many of the "absurd"—and absurdly routine—ways that tech companies invade our personal lives, influence our behavior, ignore our interests, and enforce their own values. Here's a sample from their long list of examples:

> A for-profit service tracks and sells prescription data. An app was proposed to "watch" for suicidal intentions on social media. A vibrator maker tracked its users' sex lives without disclosing it was doing so. The collection of DNA data seems ripe, and possibly already exploited, for abuse. An app to help women track their periods sells that data to aggregators. . . . The gyroscopes that track the motion of smartphones turn out to be potentially usable for speech recognition. Samsung TVs were found to be eavesdropping on people watching them. An Uber executive revealed at a party that the company's "God View" includes a remarkable amount of information about drivers and passengers[, and that] famously led Uber to write about its knowing when passengers were having one-night stands. A school used the cameras in laptops it distributed to spy on its students.[16]

Even though they all share the smart label, different types of smart tech are often treated as if they were (totally) separate from each other. The smart watch you wear, the smart home you live in, and the smart city you inhabit are rarely looked at together. Rather than analyzing them as pieces of a unified system, these connections are severed, as if smart tech operating in different places is somehow unrelated. This is ironic since the explicit goal of many major tech companies like Cisco and Google is to plug everything and everybody into a single meganetwork—a "system of systems"—which is, of course, constructed and controlled by them. IBM calls their project the "Smarter Planet," which they boldly claim "was not merely the announcement of a new strategy, but an assertion of a new world view," thus showing quite clearly the scope of their ambitions.[17]

Against this type of disjointed analysis, I argue there are shared interests and imperatives that influence the design as well as use of smart tech across different types, scales, and spaces. In other words, instead of seeing these technologies as discrete and unrelated, we should see them as parts of a powerful, yet still emerging technopolitical regime of digital capitalism. Only then can we really grapple with their impacts on society.

This book focuses on three particular spaces where this regime is being built: the smart self, smart home, and smart city. Each space has undergone a smart shock in recent years. That is, they have been subjected to a rapid, widespread, large-scale wave of smartification. The creation of a smart society is well underway.

By uncovering the technopolitics of smart tech, we will see how their impacts go far beyond the usual set of concerns about privacy intrusions and cybersecurity breaches. They are sophisticated tools that amplify the power that corporations and governments wield over our lives. They are transformative technologies that are being used to shape society in profound ways. Indeed, these impacts have caused some serious soul searching among a growing number of executives, entrepreneurs, and engineers in Silicon Valley who have helped create the smart system we must now contend with.

For example, the former vice president of user growth at Facebook, Chamath Palihapitiya, lamented during a public talk in 2017, "Your behaviors, you don't realize it, but you are being programmed. It was unintentional, but now you got to decide how much you are willing to give up."[18] While executives might sheepishly say, "My bad," much of the consciousness-raising in tech firms is coming from the bottom as workers respond to the fact that "if you're going to work at one of the companies where you have so much influence in the world, you have almost an obligation to think about how much power you have, and what you'll do it with," as a former Google programmer told the journalist Clive Thompson.[19]

Technology Doesn't Want Anything; People Do

It is easy to treat technology as an extrahuman force with its own wants, purposes, and intentions, much as we do with things like "the market" and "globalization." This view, known as technological determinism, is crystallized in the oft-repeated slogan, "Information wants to be free." Many commonly held beliefs about technology are deterministic. Since this chapter is about how we should understand technopolitics, it's important to address a major—and majorly misguided yet seductive—way people tend to think about technology. Consider the following three beliefs.[20]

First, technology is separate from society and out of our control. It is an autonomous agent or force of nature, which acts on its own. It has desires, plans, and objectives. It is a beast that cannot be tamed, and as such, any attempts to manage and guide technology are bound to backfire. We should therefore adapt our lives to innovation rather than resist it.

Second, technology develops in a linear fashion: one thing after another. Technical advancements—from stone tools to silicon chips and beyond—happen according to a rational and unbending order. Humans are conduits for the spirit of invention. If there is competition between different technologies, the winner is successful because it is objectively the best option.

Third, technology is, throughout history and today, (almost) always a liberating force for human empowerment. Technology leads to more freedom, more wealth, and better lives. It is the main cause of human well-being and the solution to all problems. The highway of innovation leads to progress and prosperity. There is only one way to drive: forward.

These beliefs have a pervasive influence, popping up all over the place. These ideas are present anytime somebody claims that technology is just a neutral tool or when any criticism of technology is dismissed as primitive Luddism. But where tech determinism thrives is in the popular writings and TED talks of futurists and "thought leaders." Such beliefs channel the Borg from *Star Trek*: "Resistance is a futile."[21]

Deterministic rhetoric is so common as to be cliché, but that does not detract from its potency. Convincing people that the present can only exist and the future can only unfold in one way is a powerful tactic. Of course, it's just a coincidence that the *one way* happens to fit the values and visions of technopolitical oligarchs like large corporations and venture capitalists. Tech determinism easily shifts into self-fulfilling prophecy. It removes human agency from the equation, while also warning people that they better get out the way, get on board, or get run over by the unstoppable march of progress. A hard-line version of determinism even insists that technological change, and therefore social change, *will* happen in a certain way because it *must* happen that way. It is fate as foretold by the futurist's crystal ball. There is no alternative.

Determinism is not only a wrong way of thinking about technology; it's dangerous because it only appears to separate technology from its human and social dimensions. This means certain people can continue making technologies that reflect their values and impact our lives, but now they are hidden by the facade of determinism. They no longer face the threat of accountability. After all, if technology just happens, then nobody is to blame. Better yet, if it happens because that's the natural, divine, only, and best possible way for it to happen, then nobody can complain.

Tech determinism makes intuitive sense because technology— and *the future*—feels like a thing that just happens to us. The vast majority of us are disconnected from the design and development of new technologies. We don't see the various decisions, disagreements, and detours that are part of every technology. The successful designs that see the light of day seem to follow a natural evolution or just spring forth fully formed from the mind of a great innovator. At least, these are the stories told to us over and over by marketing teams, tech journalists, and hagiographic biographers. As Meghan O'Gieblyn deftly writes, "For most consumers—who learn about new technologies only when they brighten the windows of an Apple store or after they've already gone viral—it's easy to imagine that technological progress is indeed dictated by a kind of divine logic; that machines are dropped into our lives on their own accord, like strange gifts from the gods."[22]

It is comforting to think that technology is a force for good, shepherding us to a better world. Tech determinism offers simple explanations for complex processes. But in doing so, it obscures all the ways that technology is an intensely human and social phenomenon. It is the result of cultural norms, political choices, and economic systems—not its own independent autonomy. Moreover, technological development isn't a smooth, straight road. It is a network of alleyways filled with dead-ends and pot-holes. The failures and false starts in the history of technology are plentiful.[23] Some technologies succeed over others because of a host of criteria and conditions. Perhaps designers have good reason for choosing one value (like cost) over another (like safety) when making a technology, but that doesn't mean the choice is any less subjective or variable. One group's idea of what is "good" or "optimal" is not the same as everybody else's idea. There are always multiple ways to develop or use a technology.

At best, determinism muddles our thinking about tech and society. At worst, determinism breeds passivity. If we are to understand who makes smart tech, what drives its design, and how it impacts our lives, then we have to break free of tech determinism. We have to question, not merely accept, the politics of smart tech. All tech is a contingent creation: it can be built in different ways, with different purposes, and to achieve different goals—or just not built at all. When we lack a critical technopolitics of design and instead rely on deterministic explanations, however, we end up securing the authority of executives, engineers, and entrepreneurs who get to decide what kind of tech will be created. This group has grown comfortable with its outsized influence and wealth.

A useful heuristic for political analysis comes from the late Tony Benn, who was a long-serving member of Parliament in the United Kingdom. Benn famously came up with what he called "five little democratic questions" that should be posed to any powerful person or institution: What power have you got? Where did you get it from? In whose interests do you exercise it? To whom are you accountable? How can we get rid of you? Benn concluded that the last question might be the most important because "if you cannot get rid of the people who govern you, you do not live in a democratic system."[24]

These questions are a framework for critically analyzing politics. We should thus pose them to the individuals, corporations, and governments that are creating the smart society we inhabit, especially considering that the technopolitical power they wield will end up having more real influence over our lives and society than many politicians ever do.[25] With Benn's five questions as guidance, we can confront the politics of smart tech.

Coming Up Next

The chapters that follow will be a tour of the smart tech that has become a pervasive and invasive part of society. I discuss some, but certainly not all, of smart tech's impacts on our lives today and its implications for our lives tomorrow. I also highlight many, but again not all, of the powerful interests that direct how smart tech is designed and why it is used. I largely focus on the different ways that smart tech is harmful, risky, and unjust (because the tech industry, media, and government don't need any more help singing the praises of smartification). But this critical framing does not crop out a world of good just to highlight a selection of worries. I do not even come close to exhausting all the examples of how smart tech impacts people in egregious ways. No book can be everything, but I hope this one is an eye-opening and thought-provoking guide to the smart society that is emerging all around us.

In what follows, I provide plenty of examples that illustrate the larger trends, themes, and implications of smart tech and digital capitalism. They all offer something to grab onto, and ground what would otherwise be abstract points about the technopolitics of power and profit. After all, it's hard to understand the realities of digital capitalism without talking about real technologies, real people, and real consequences. Yet at the same time, I caution the reader not to get too focused on the collection of anecdotes. The main point is what these examples mean and why they matter. Moreover, just as this book aims to tie together a range of technologies and topics, so too does its analysis synthesize my research and writing on the subjects of technopolitics, digital capitalism, and smart tech. For the sake of style and readability, I don't always explicitly point out when I'm building on my original contributions to the field, as academics are taught to do. Nevertheless, my extensive academic work, even when it blends into the background, forms the foundations of this book.

In terms of what to expect, the rest of the book dives into the nitty-gritty details of smart tech—and what we can do about it.

The three chapters of part I explore both imperatives and the political economic system they emerge from. That is, they provide us with a deeper, albeit more abstract, view of collection, control, and digital capitalism.

Chapter 2 explains how data has become a central element of contemporary capitalism. Data has, in quick fashion, gone from largely being the concern of research scientists and policy wonks to now being treated as a form of capital. When data becomes capital, we end up with a surplus of smart systems and

platforms that are built to track every person, place, and thing—
and stream all that data directly to corporations.

Chapter 3 describes how society is filled with control systems
that have colonized everyday life. They watch and track people
by capturing data about specific aspects and actions. They use
various metrics to judge, rate, and rank people. They establish
checkpoints that regulate access and enforce exclusion. By analyzing the way control operates at different scales, we can draw
links between smart technologies that were before thought of as
separate. The innocuous is enfolded with the menacing.

Chapter 4 offers ten theses about the operations and outcomes of digital capitalism. Contrary to the frequently repeated
mantra that Silicon Valley start-ups are revolutionary and smart
tech is unlike anything that came before, the rise of the digital
age is more often an update to old forms of political economic
dynamics. We are not witnessing a disruptive break from history
but rather a new way of repackaging, reproducing, and revitalizing the social structures as well as economic relations that came
before. Each thesis is a provocative statement drawn from critically studying how the smart society is developing. When taken
together, they provide a diagnosis of digital capitalism.

The three chapters of part II each focus on a different scale of
smart tech.

Chapter 5 shows how smart tech is used to measure, monitor, manage, and monetize all aspects of our lives. The rise of
the smart self is based on much more than just people choosing
to track themselves. The most important consequences of the
smart self arise from what others do with our data and how they
direct our behavior, whether we want them to or not. We are
already subjected to a wide range of technologies designed to

track, profile, and manage us. We don't have to rely on radical examples. We just have to look around.

Chapter 6 moves into the smart home, where Silicon Valley start-ups and legacy manufacturers alike are aggressively pushing new devices, appliances, and services. Whereas the dumb fridge just keeps food cold, the smart fridge also keeps track of what you eat, how often, and when. Under digital capitalism, our devices are not just commodities; they are a means of producing data. By monitoring every interaction and communicating with each other, smart appliances can collect valuable data about your habits and preferences. For businesses, smart tech provides a window into private domestic spaces.

Chapter 7 takes us to the city level. The city has become something of a natural habitat for smart tech. It's in the urban environment where these systems have space to grow big, stretch out, and flex their might. There are sensor networks to watch the city, algorithms to analyze the city, control rooms to govern the city, and plenty of other smart systems that are designed to capture every part of the city (and its inhabitants). These systems grant powerful capabilities to city governments and tech companies. Perhaps most consequentially for urban society—and the focus of this chapter—smart tech has radically shifted how the police operate. Thanks to the use of military-grade surveillance and analytics, police forces are now more like a city intelligence agency—the new CIA. Not long ago these urban systems would have only existed in the hopes and fears of speculative stories. Now they are part of our streets.

Part II, aka chapter 8, offers a framework based on three ways we can challenge digital capitalism. Redefining and redesigning the smart society won't be easy, but it is necessary. The three recommendations outlined here inform how we can go about creating a different kind of technological society. The first starts with everyday resistance to extraction and exploitation, and then argues for unmaking certain technical systems. The second begins with the need for democratizing innovation and then provides an example of how this has been attempted in the past. The third starts with oversight of the data economy and protection from data-driven harms, and then proposes treating data as a public asset that is administered for the common good.

I Drivers of Digital Capitalism

2 A Universe of Data

Many a battle will be fought over who should own, and benefit from, data.

—"Data Is Giving Rise to a New Economy," *Economist*, 2017

It's increasingly clear we live in the age of Amazon. When systems of production and distribution have major effects on how people live and work, we tend to name time periods after them. For instance, the era of capitalism that kicked off a hundred years ago is now called Fordism because of the way Ford Motor's system of mass production and mass consumption transformed the economy and society. It's not a stretch to say that in the future, the current period might be known as Amazonian. Indeed, Amazon will be a recurrent character throughout this book. That's not because I set out to write about Amazon but instead because it's impossible not to encounter Amazon again and again when studying smart tech and/or contemporary capitalism.

The online retail giant is synonymous with growth and disruption. As the scourge of brick-and-mortar shops, Amazon has been credited with gutting bookstores, shuttering small businesses, and even threatening its fellow giants like Walmart. The disruptors become the disrupted. Thus it came as a surprise to many people when Amazon announced in June 2017 that it was buying the high-end grocery chain Whole Foods for $13.7 billion. With this one deal, Amazon now owns over 460 physical stores across the United States.

This already-forgotten event in Amazon's history—because now too much happens too quickly—tells us a lot about the development of digital capitalism and the value of data.

Business analysts rushed to point out that Amazon's acquisition would give it a foothold in the grocery business and further expand its massive logistical network. These reasons all make sense when thinking about how a profitable company might keep the cash flowing by growing into new sectors. This standard commentary doesn't give us the whole picture, however. We have to remember that Amazon is not just a retailer but also a tech company, which means it has different priorities and motivations. It sees the world with cybernetic eyes.

The "big prize" in the Whole Foods deal is data.[1] Amazon already knows everything about its customers' online shopping habits. This kind of data is critical to Amazon's success. It allows the company to serve targeted recommendations, predict purchases, and optimize prices on items (sometimes changing them multiple times a day), all to get people to spend more money. Amazon is a paragon of digital capitalism. It is a fully data-driven business. In fact, Amazon's retail front is more like a side business. Its major profit engine is the cloud computing subsidiary Amazon Web Services, which made $17.46 billion in revenue during 2017—a rate that keeps growing every year—by supplying businesses and governments with their computational and database needs.[2]

By acquiring Whole Foods, Amazon now owns a treasure trove of data about people's behavior in physical stores. People shop differently online and off-line; they have different habits and make different choices. Knowing how a person behaves in a virtual store doesn't necessarily tell you how they behave in a physical one. This data is valuable, which is why grocery stores have been tracking shoppers for decades.[3] The now-ubiquitous "loyalty card"—chances are you have a few in your wallet or bag—was created as a way to collect and categorize data about customers.[4] By offering (small) discounts, customers are incentivized to sign up for a card that they scan at every checkout.

It was an ingenious innovation that allowed stores to turn faceless customers into continuously tracked profiles. Grocery stores already knew what was bought, when it was bought, and where it was bought, but now they have a better idea of who is buying and how they shop. By linking purchases to individuals, stores can build profiles that reveal people's preferences, habits, and characteristics. They turn those preferences into patterns, which fuel targeted advertisements and predictions about future spending.

Obtaining such a valuable reserve of data about shoppers was a key factor in the Amazon–Whole Foods deal. The aim is not only track us off-line and online but also track us across the digital divide by linking these two profiles.

For Amazon, stores like Whole Foods are not extracting and exploiting anywhere near as much data about customers as they could be. Even before the acquisition, Amazon had been testing ways of transforming stores into fully surveilled, datafied, automated places. In its smart stores, called Amazon Go, you scan your phone on walking in, grab your groceries, and just walk out.[5] No check out necessary; your account will be autobilled. In return for this convenience, Amazon will track your location and behavior via hundreds of small cameras throughout the store equipped with analytics software—where you browse, how long you linger, and what you pick up and put back.[6]

The idea is, essentially, to take all the real-time tracking and analytics capabilities of the internet, and apply them to the rest of the world, thus turning stores into "physical websites."[7] Early versions of this type of smart tech already exists. For years now, department stores like Nordstrom have been tracking shoppers— without their knowledge or permission—using the Wi-Fi signals from smartphones.[8] Hotels and high-end shops also use facial recognition to identify VIP customers who deserve special treatment and known troublemakers to kick out.[9] Fast-food chains in the United States and China are now starting to use facial recognition kiosks to identify "loyal" customers, make menu recommendations, and allow payment with face scans rather than card swipes.[10] All this smart tech is just the beginning, though. "A global race to automate stores is underway among several of the world's top retailers and small tech start-ups," according to the *New York Times*.[11]

Amazon is poised to lead the way in building even smarter stores that monitor every person, thing, and action. The smart store is a lean, mean, data-collecting machine. Decked out with "computer vision, deep learning algorithms, and sensor fusion," the smart store won't just recognize famous faces but will identify everybody and access their personal profile too.[12] It knows you better than you know yourself. It never forgets, analyzes everything, and predicts your habits. Amazon can send personalized, in-store advertisements directly to your phone. It can more effectively nudge you, upsell you, and predict when you will buy certain things.

In the future, Amazon might even offer to send you the items it has decided you will want. After all, Amazon lets you sign up for a subscription service that automatically delivers goods like toothpaste and toilet paper. With more data, the smart store—like the smart home and smart city—can be more than automatic; it can have agency. The slogan could be, "Amazon Choice: Toss away the grocery list. We already know what you want!"

How appropriate that under digital capitalism, the smart store becomes a model for society. It's based on the same trade-off at the heart of much "innovation" now: in exchange for allowing Amazon to perfect the tools of total surveillance, behavioral modification, and value extraction, we get a somewhat more convenient experience.

Data as Capital

The Amazon–Whole Foods deal is a just one example of how the imperative of data collection plays a major role in many business decisions and technological designs. Similar cases of cash-for-data deals abound, like when IBM bought the Weather Company in 2015 for reportedly $2 billion to obtain its mountains of data and infrastructure for collecting data.[13] The valuable data in this case is not only about atmospheric conditions but also the geolocation points collected by the Weather Channel apps installed on most people's phones. The multitude of apps that track our geolocation do so with startling accuracy, hundreds or thousands of times a day, thus revealing detailed information about our daily movements. Does a flashlight app really need access to our location? It does when this data fuels a market for location-targeted advertising that was estimated to be worth $21 *billion* in 2018.[14]

Such cases illustrate an important lesson about our smart society: just as we expect corporations to be profit driven, we should now expect them to be data driven. That is, they are motivated by a deep need to hoard as much data as possible.

At a public talk in early 2017, Andrew Ng, an artificial intelligence researcher who has held top positions at Google, Baidu, and Coursera, was explicit about the primacy of data collection: "At large companies, sometimes we launch products not for the revenue, but for the data. We actually do that quite often . . . and we monetize the data through a different product."[15] Ng's admission aligns perfectly with a general rule outlined by sociologists Marion Fourcade and Kieran Healy: "It does not matter that the amounts [of data] collected may vastly exceed a firm's imaginative reach or analytic grasp. The assumption is that it will eventually be useful, i.e., valuable. . . . Contemporary organizations are both culturally impelled by the data imperative and powerfully equipped with the tools to enact it."[16]

This insatiable hunger for data arises from the fact that data is now a form of capital, just like money and machinery.[17] Data is both valuable and value creating. It is central to the production of new systems and services. It is essential for companies to extract more profit from—and exercise more power over—people, places, and processes. In short, as I first argued in an article for the journal *Big Data and Society*, the collection and circulation of data as capital is now a core feature of contemporary capitalism.[18] Meeting the demands of this data imperative has been a prime motivation for how capital creates and uses technology.

Not long ago, companies simply deleted data or chose not to collect it because paying for storage did not seem like a good investment. Now, though, companies are clamoring to collect data—as much as they can, wherever they can. Their data banks can never be too big. For the increasing number of sectors embracing the "data economy" or "digital economy," deleting data because of storage costs would be like burning piles of money or dumping barrels of oil down the drain because renting a warehouse was too much trouble.

It seems that every industry across the economy is now pivoting toward datafication as their primary business. Even the old paragons of capitalism recognize they have to follow Amazon's lead. As the *Economist* noted in a cover article on the value of data, "Industrial giants such as GE and Siemens now sell themselves as data firms."[19] Similarly, in November 2018, Ford's CEO announced that the company's revenue will soon rely on monetizing and selling the data it collects from the "100 million people" driving Ford vehicles.[20] These industries now see data—detailed data about our personal lives and private spaces—as a source of "pure profit." They are only heeding the call of digital capitalism.

The existence of start-ups that seemingly do nothing but burn through money and gather loads of data, while bringing in little revenue and netting huge losses, is confusing from a traditional business standpoint. Even more confusing is the fact that these firms are often given massive valuations by venture capitalists and are acquired for equally large sums of money. How can a company have negative earnings yet be seen by investors as worth many millions or billions of dollars? It's all about the data. Or put differently, "The data is the business model," as former Amazon executive John Rossman wrote.[21]

Data is used to generate value in a number of different ways. Here are six major ones.[22] I will explore these and other ways further in the rest of the book:

1. Data is used to *profile and target* people. Many business models and services in data capitalism are based on the value proposition that knowing more about people will, in some way, translate to more profit. Internet-based companies often make their revenue by serving personalized advertisements. Retailers can charge different prices based on the customer's characteristics. Political consultants analyze data to decide who is susceptible to certain kinds of messaging and influence.

2. Data is used to *optimize* systems. It can make machines more efficient, workers more productive, and platforms more frictionless. By showing how to eliminate waste and do more with less, data translates into big savings. This might mean an industrial manufacturer installing sensors on mechanical systems or a management consultant using algorithmic analysis to assess how a city government should run its programs.

3. Data is used to *manage* things. This essentially boils down to the relationships between knowledge and power: they are in a relationship with each; they require each other. Here data is a digital, formal, mobile, machine-readable form of knowledge. The idea is that by amassing data about a thing, then the ability to control that thing is enhanced. This might be as mundane as a person keeping track of their diet and exercise so they can manage their health. Or it might be as complex as an engineer overseeing the traffic patterns of a city so they can manage how millions of people move through space.

4. Data is used to *model* probabilities. With enough data covering a wide range of variables over a period of the time—fed to the right algorithms and data analysts—the promise made

by many highly valued companies is that they can predict the future. In reality, these "predictions" are better thought of as probabilities, but they are frequently treated more as crystal balls. The areas where data-driven predictions are made go way beyond forecasting the weather, such as "predictive policing" systems that create "heat lists" and "hot spots" that name who and where has a high likelihood of criminal activity.

5. Data is used to *build* stuff. Digital systems and services are often built around data: they require data to operate, put to use existing data, and collect new data. A platform like Uber couldn't exist without real-time data about drivers and passengers. As more devices become "smart," they also become data driven and internet connected to facilitate the flow of data to and from the device. Advances in artificial intelligence and machine learning are fueled by mountains of data used to train these systems.

6. Data is used to *grow* the value of assets. Things like buildings, infrastructure, vehicles, and machinery are depreciating assets. They lose value over time as the forces of entropy—or wear and tear—take their toll. Yet upgrading assets with smart tech that collects data about their use helps combat the normal cycle of deterioration. They become, as financier Stuart Kirk states, "more adaptive and responsive, thereby extending their useful lives."[23] Rather than depreciating, smartified assets can maintain and gain value. Or if they don't grow value, at least data can slow its decay.

Masters of the Data Universe

Fulfilling the imperative of collection involves more than just passively gathering data; it means actively creating data. The common term data mining is misleading. A more apt term would be *data manufacturing*. Data is not out there waiting to be discovered as if it already exists in the world like crude oil and raw ore.[24] Data is created about the world by people using technical processes. The framing of data as a natural resource—"the new oil"—that is everywhere and free for the taking reinforces regimes of data extraction.

In a video promoting its idea of "smart data," Siemens, the largest industrial manufacturer in Europe, tells us what the world looks like through the lens of digital capitalism: "We live in a universe of data that gains not only in volume, but importance, every day. The question of how to generate business value from it becomes more and more essential to us. We need to understand that data is everywhere, and it is generated every second of the day. We need to understand data as an asset and turn it into a value."[25] Other tech companies express similar views of the world. The global tech company IBM recently declared, "Everything is made of data these days."[26]

It is not a coincidence that data has been recast as an omnipresent resource right at the time when there is so much to gain for whoever can lay claim to that data and capitalize on its value. Those who possess data are put in a position of special access and authority over the world. Flows of data correspond to flows of power and profit. Thus the alchemy of datafication promises to produce an infinite reserve of both. At the same time, the rhetoric of data universality reframes *everything* as within the domain of digital capitalism. No system can be truly totalizing and universal, not even one that can potentially turn any person, place, or process into a source of value. But that has not stopped the forces of data capital from trying.

Even though much of our lives has already become digitized and datafied, the smart society is still in its early phases. According

to the champions of digital capitalism, one of the major imped-
iments to its development is that many companies do not yet
"fully appreciate" that "their data is their single biggest asset."[27]
Simply put, companies are not yet collecting and capitalizing on
enough data. This isn't because they are only gathering small
amounts of data—only what's needed, and nothing more—but
rather because the amount harvested can always be bigger. The
data imperative isn't based on meeting a quota of data collected;
it is a never-ending quest to amass, hoard, and exploit data.

The imperative of collection is based on a vicious feedback
loop: smart tech not only demands constant flows of data to
operate, it is also the machinery for manufacturing the universe
of data. By harnessing the power of smart tech, corporations like
Amazon, Google, and many others that we will encounter aim
to become the new "masters of the universe," to borrow a phrase
that Tom Wolfe used to describe the titans of Wall Street in the
1980s.[28]

3 Control Freaks

Simultaneously material and ideological . . . transitions from the comfortable old hierarchical dominations to the scary new networks I have called the informatics of domination.

—Donna Haraway, "A Cyborg Manifesto," 1985

Not long ago, the apartment complex where I lived at the time decided to upgrade its security by installing mechanical gates at every entrance. Opening these gates required a plastic fob with a chip inside, which worked like a keycard (by pressing it against a receiver at the pedestrian gate) and garage door opener (by clicking a button for the vehicle gate). The new electronic entrances seemed unnecessary. The complex was in a safe part of town, right next to the university where I was studying, and if somebody wanted to wander in to sit in the sunny courtyard or drop in on a friend, then more power to them. At most, I thought the gates would just be a minor inconvenience: one more step on my way home, another thing hanging on my key chain.

I was wrong. The complex did not ensure that the security gates worked well after installing them. So for weeks my fob would only open the entrance part of the time, effectively locking me out of my home, stranding me on the sidewalk, until a fellow resident came along and opened the gate from the inside. Or if I were feeling adventurous, I could attempt to climb the concrete wall and metal gate, which meant risking injury and being stopped for trespassing. Since the arbitrary access did not affect the complex's managers, they were slow to fix the problem. In response, people began trying to prop the gate open. This was no small feat: the gate was heavy and spring-loaded to slam shut. Even when people succeeded, employees at the complex were instructed to remove any props.

It didn't matter that the security system was obtrusive or the people it was intended to safeguard didn't want its protection. The system's integrity had to be maintained and its commands had to be obeyed. Better to keep everybody out than to possibly let in the wrong person. Better to have total lockdown than even the appearance that things were out of control.

The other residents and I were forced to experience the exact frustrating situation that the philosopher Gilles Deleuze described in his prescient 1992 essay, "Postscript on the Societies of Control":

> [Imagine] a city where one would be able to leave one's apartment, one's street, one's neighborhood, thanks to one's (dividual) electronic card that raises a given barrier; but the card could just as easily be rejected on a given day or between certain hours; what counts is not the barrier but the computer that tracks each person's position—licit or illicit—and effects a universal modulation.[1]

When Deleuze originally wrote this example it sounded like cyberpunk science fiction, but it sure didn't feel like fiction when I had to deal with a temperamental gate.

Compared to other possible consequences of control, the gate glitching was only relatively annoying. But it illustrates the imperative of control that colonizes everyday life, filling it with checkpoints that regulate access and enforce exclusion. My experience of the gate wasn't merely a strange coincidence— considering that I was working on this book, when I wasn't locked out on the streets—because these technological situations are *now normal* features of the world. Even though Deleuze outlined his theory of control almost thirty years ago, it remains one of the best ways to understand the operations and implications of smart tech.[2]

Forms of Power

Before explaining Deleuze's theory, let's set the stage with a brief history of power in human society. It will be helpful to keep these different kinds of power in mind as I explore the impacts of smart tech and mechanics of digital capitalism. After all, technopolitics is the analysis of the power of technology and technology of power.

When most people think of power, they likely think in terms of force. In this form, power is the ability to make people do what you say—to obey a command, follow a rule, and/or change their behavior—usually by the threat of punishment. This kind of power has been called "sovereign power" because it is how monarchs and lords wield power over their subjects.[3] But today we can just think of it in terms of fear and force. It's power backed up by authority and assault. The police and parents both wield this type of power. Do what they say or else you'll be in trouble; in some cases, that means being grounded or imprisoned, and in other cases, it means being spanked or shot. For much of human history, this is the main way power has been exercised in society. Without a doubt, it is still a tragically common part of life for many people, but power also takes other less direct, more diffused, yet still influential and violent forms.

A second form of power is what social theorist Michel Foucault called *biopower*, but we can call it by a simpler name: discipline.[4] Power works in this way by instilling certain ways of thinking and behaving into people. People internalize these beliefs, habits, and norms. They are then shaped into certain kinds of people (or "subjects") by institutions like schools, workplaces, and prisons. In this form, power is the ability to decide what is good and normal—that is, how people should be disciplined—and establish institutions and methods to discipline people accordingly. Foucault writes, "The old power of death that symbolized sovereign power was now carefully supplanted by the administration of bodies and the calculated management of life."[5]

Sovereign power is exercised by issuing commands, threatening force, and carrying out punishment. Discipline operates by fostering ways of living, rejecting "deviant" lifestyles, and watching people to make sure they behave appropriately. As good disciplined subjects, we have a voice in our head telling us to act right. We police ourselves and those around us by making sure we/they fit in with social norms. If somebody steps out of line, we gossip about and ostracize them from social life. If the offense is serious enough, we resort to the old ways of removing them from society via prisons and asylums.

The third form of power is control. Rather than threatening people with violence or shaping who they are, control works by setting parameters for what's allowed and establishing checkpoints that regulate actions. People can act freely within those parameters as long as they allow themselves to be tracked at all times. To put this differently, discipline abhors too much individuality. People need to conform to the model of a good student, good worker, good citizen, and so on. There is no tolerance for deviance and abnormality. Whereas, as surveillance scholars Patrick O'Byrne and Dave Holmes explain in terms of gender and sexuality, control operates on different principles:

> Deleuze's society of control permits a nearly endless expression of individuality: the macho-man, the gay man, the metro-sexual, et cetera, the lip-stick lesbian, the bull-dyke, the blue-jean femme, et cetera. As part of this, however, each individual must render him/herself open and exposed at all times. Be gay, for example, but do so while ensuring that your sexuality is fully exposed to [sexually transmitted disease] and HIV management workers. In the new social system, one's every movement must be known, tracked, and analyzed.[6]

The symbol of disciplinary power is the panopticon: a structure built in such a way that you know you could always be watched, but you never know when or if you are being watched, so you always behave as if you are. Discipline trades on equal parts paranoia, guilt, and shame.

The symbol of control, however, is the computer network that invisibly, constantly, and continuously records every action, and rejects any action that does not fit with its code. Control systems do not rely on mere threats of surveillance. They follow through on monitoring, judging, and inhibiting your freedom if you run afoul of their parameters. Unlike the panopticon, it doesn't matter if you know about the system. In fact, it's probably better (for the system) if you are unaware of its operations.

For a mundane example of these different forms of power in action, consider how each one can be used to prevent a child from opening their presents before Christmas. First, under sovereign power, the parent could hide the presents and then tell the kid that they will be in trouble if they go snooping for the gifts. If the kid disobeys, then they are punished in some way. The more authoritarian the parent, the more severe the command and punishment.

Second, under disciplinary power, the parent keeps the presents under the tree in plain view. But since the parent can't always be around to watch the presents, the parent instills good behavior in the kid by putting an "Elf on a Shelf" by the presents. The kid is taught that the Elf is always watching and reporting their behavior to Santa. If they are bad, then Santa will put them on the naughty list and take away their presents. With the threat of constant surveillance, the kid polices their own behavior and acts like a "good child."

Third, under control power, the parent puts the presents in a smart box that is equipped with cameras, sensors, actuators, and Wi-Fi connection. Once activated, the box records motion such as somebody picking it up and shaking it. Any attempt to tamper with the box is registered as a security breach. An automatic alert is then sent to the parent's smartphone, along with a video of the intruder. The only way to get the presents is by entering a password in the app, which unlocks the box.

Three Parts of Control

In practice, these three forms of power are not totally separate from each other. They blend together and coexist. Control is the most relevant one for our purposes—so the next few sections will dive deeper into how control operates—but we will see many cases of how force and discipline are also channeled through smart tech. Even though Deleuze was writing before the things we call "smart" existed, his theory tells us a lot about how these systems operate and impact our lives. According to Deleuze, there are three key parts to control systems: rhizomes, dividuals, and passwords.

Rhizomes

Smart tech can be hard to wrap our heads around. A common device like the Amazon Alexa is an immensely complex system of data flows, cloud servers, algorithmic analysis, communication protocols, user interfaces, human labor, rare earth metals, and many other components and layers.[7] These systems are digital, virtual, and informational, but also material, mechanical, biological, and spatial. They are contained in handheld devices, but also sprawling networks. We cannot easily draw boundaries around such systems, nor can we see all the ways they are interconnected. Many of the systems that we interact with—and interact with us—are often hidden from sight and mind.

We experience parts of them at the point of interaction, like when tapping a debit card at the store, but that interface is only the tip of a submerged system. This invisibility is by design. Mark Weiser, a pioneer of ubiquitous computing, famously stated, "The most profound technologies are those that disappear. They weave themselves into the fabric of everyday life until they are indistinguishable from it."[8] In other words, they become the infrastructure of contemporary life; we rely on and take them for granted. We tend not to notice them unless they breakdown or deny us access.[9] If we are going to actively engage with smart tech, then we need different ways to think about how they exist and operate as systems.

Deleuze and his collaborator Félix Guattari offer an interesting way to conceptualize these underlying, ubiquitous systems in terms of *rhizomes*.[10] They borrow this idea from botany, where a rhizome is a type of plant: a mass of tangled roots that is usually subterranean, sending roots and shoots from its various nodes, which spread through the ground and break through the surface. When seen aboveground, the different shoots seem separate, like individual trees in a forest, but in reality, they are all tied together through an invisible network of connections and interfaces. It is one entangled system appearing to be many individual things.

One of the most striking examples of a botanical rhizome is known as Pando (Latin for "I spread") or the Trembling Giant. This enormous grove of quaking aspens in Utah is a single living organism. Even though it looks like a normal forest, albeit especially beautiful, according to Slate, "Every tree—or stem, technically—is genetically identical, and the whole forest is linked by a single root system."[11] Pando is the world's heaviest organism (over forty thousand stems) and among the world's oldest living things (eighty thousand years). It has become so large and survived so long because it is constantly regenerating and reproducing itself.

Similarly, we can see the rapid growth of a technological rhizome through the ongoing effort to connect everything together into integrated, expansive, smart systems. This trend is also known as the Internet of Things or the Internet of Everything. In her famous 1985 essay, "A Cyborg Manifesto," Haraway foresaw how such a system could subsume the world: "No objects, spaces, or bodies are sacred in themselves; any component can be interfaced with any other if the proper standard, the proper code, can be constructed for processing signals in a common language."[12] Today we are seeing attempts to make this vision come true. And in the process, competing corporate alliances are fighting a war over whose standards will succeed—that is, the technical protocols that allow things and data to be interconnected—thus giving its creators the power to shape and dominate the global rhizome.

The rhizomatic smart systems spread and creep, becoming massive and sprawling, while reproducing the interests and imperatives they represent. Uprooting a large rhizome is a difficult task. You can try to shear off parts of it, but more stems will emerge elsewhere from the mass of roots. Rhizomes have no distinct boundaries, and no starting or ending points; rather, they emanate from multiple directions and intensities. Their actions can be subtle and stark, continuous and intermittent. Their rhizomatic nature means their impacts are dispersed and unequal: for some, the systems channel and amplify their capacities, while for others, the systems surveil and control their lives.

Dividuals

New methods of monitoring can constantly harvest data, yet they do so in hyperspecific ways. For example, no sensor is actually designed to absorb and record data about everything that happens around it. Instead, each sensor is designed to monitor specific things: the ambient temperature, how many times a door is opened, the face-shaped objects in its visual area, or whatever else. When targeted at people's attributes and actions, the ability for smart tech to hone in on a specific factor and excise it from the surrounding context turns us into what Deleuze calls *dividuals*, or divided individuals: beings able to be divided into any number of pieces that are separated, surveilled, and scrutinized.

The process of dividualization is as if our self—our body, behaviors, identities, and characteristics—was refracted through a prism. Like a beam of white light that is broken into a rainbow, each part of the whole is displayed. As smart tech becomes more advanced and more pervasive, we are blown apart into increasingly more streams of data. We are atomized by the prism for the purpose of accumulation, analysis, and actionable insights.

Smart tech enhances the ability to take one attribute, action, or category, and make it representative of the whole person.

That one thing becomes all that matters. The biometric lock is only concerned with your fingerprint. The GPS keeps track of your geospatial coordinates. The health wristband records your vital signs. We now have a thousand identities, each represented by a thousand data points collected by a thousand devices. "The human body," as sociologists Kevin Haggerty and Richard Ericson explain, "is broken down by being abstracted from its territorial setting. It is then reassembled in different settings through a series of data flows. The result is a decorporealized body, a 'data double' of pure virtuality."[13] While the dividualized self exists in the virtual space of databases, the effects of how that data double is extracted and employed are extremely material. The abstraction of datafication, as I argue in the next chapter, is itself a form of violence.

Living in a smart society means always being divided, being further dividualized. The units of analysis get smaller and more precise, as the ability to capture different kinds of data is refined. Dividuals are easier to administer than individuals. They fit better into databases and processors. The system can finally cut to the point and focus on what it really cares about: not the person, but the collection and flow of data from the person.

Passwords

As we interact with various systems of control—and they interact with us—we encounter checkpoints, which mediate access and restriction, freedom and constraint. Each checkpoint requires what Deleuze described as a *password* to move through it. These passwords are products of being dividualized; they are parts that permit the whole to move freely. They are like keys, but are not always physical objects made to fit a single lock. In addition to the code for unlocking a phone or logging into a computer, other common passwords can be the keycard needed to open an electronic door, personal identification number used to purchase things, or visa that allows you to not be deported.

Life is filled with these checkpoints, and possessing the right passwords is necessary for navigating a control society. "The password is able to garner, or restrict, such freedom because an array of ubiquitous and unseen mechanisms continuously monitors the user's activity," write O'Byrne and Holmes.[14] The rhizome, dividual, and password come together to enact control.

When everything matches up, when everything works smoothly and efficiently, we have no reason to pause. In the buzzword of Silicon Valley, the interfaces are *frictionless*. These control systems are designed not to be noticed until—rightly or wrongly—one decides your password is invalid. Then their presence and power become bluntly apparent when the screen alerts you: Access denied. Transaction declined. Password rejected. A control system that works perfectly and one that is prone to malfunction can both end up having effects that are identical. It can be impossible to parse out who or what to blame. Did I do something wrong? Has the system failed? What rituals are required to fix the problem?

As smart tech acquires further control over physical objects like doors, homes, and cities, there is little to no opportunity for the dialogue that is a hallmark of human relations. Instead, these interactions are at their core rigid and commanding rather than communicative. The consequences of control result not from the "unforced force of the better argument," or even coaxing and cajoling, but instead by force alone.[15] These systems extend the power of their programmers over space and time. The checkpoint enforces their authority while also removing them from the interaction. You cannot argue with an algorithm or debate with data. You only have your password and the hope that everything is in working order.

Command and Conquer

In short, control works through various, sprawling, connected, hidden systems, which monitor people by breaking them down into data points that can be recorded, analyzed, and assessed in real time, so that their freedom of access, action, and so on, can be regulated via checkpoints and passwords.

While Deleuze may have intended his theory to be a self-preventing prophecy—sounding the alarm about new forms of modulation and manipulation—it is now recognizable as the shadow side of smart tech. For some people, the smart society is a dream they eagerly want to turn into reality, while for others it is more like a nightmare, which seems to have interpreted Deleuze's description of "societies of control" as a blueprint for technopolitics. These systems exist on a spectrum, with meritorious or merely creepy technologies connected with deeply disturbing ones.[16] The innocuous is enfolded with the menacing. The difference comes down to whose interests are represented, what imperatives drive it, and how are the impacts felt. In the context of digital capitalism, the distribution of dreams and nightmares are highly uneven and highly concentrated.

4 Ten Theses on Digital Capitalism

> The smarter enterprise . . . will force economic growth and it will
> force societal progress.
> —Ginni Rometty, IBM chair and CEO, speech at IBM InterConnect,
> 2013

To orient our exploration of smart homes, smart cities, and smart fill-in-the-blanks, I outline a series of theses about the operations and outcomes of digital capitalism. They are conclusions drawn from critically studying how our technological society is developing. Each thesis stands alone as a statement about the technopolitics of today and tomorrow, if we do not change course. When taken together, they provide a diagnosis of digital capitalism, which builds from and contributes to a growing body of research about the relationship between data-driven surveillance, internet platforms, and capitalism.[1]

I call it *digital* capitalism merely to mean capitalism with digital technologies. It's a broad term that aims to incorporate other modifiers that have become popular without also being constrained by the narrow focuses or idiosyncratic features of some of these other concepts. Consider two of the most influential works: Nick Srnicek's critical analysis of "platform capitalism" is aimed at explaining how platforms like Facebook and Uber have emerged, how they work (e.g., network effects), and how they became dominant in the twenty-first-century economy.[2] Similarly, Shoshana Zuboff's blockbuster book on "surveillance capitalism" takes an in-depth look at the business model and existential threat of tech companies like Google, which are obsessed with harvesting and monetizing behavioral data.[3]

While both of these works offer useful analyses and cases, my approach differs from them in varying ways. Unlike Srnicek, my focus is on more than just platforms; rather, I examine the political economy of a much wider array of data-driven, network-connected, and automated systems. Unlike Zuboff, I do not consider the centrality of surveillance in capitalism to be "a rogue mutation," as she calls it, of a more normal, socially just version of capitalism.[4] We're not dealing with a technopolitical system that is outside capitalism or an aberration of it. In many ways, it's just variations of the same old capitalism, but now running on some new hardware and software. And that brings me to the first thesis.

Thesis One

The operations of capital are adapting to the digital age, while also still maintaining the same essential features of exclusion, extraction, and exploitation.[5]

Smart tech—and the people who design and use it—does not exist in a vacuum. All technology is a product of its environment. It absorbs, and often amplifies, features of the dominant cultural values, social structures, economic systems, and political regimes.

A recent crop of excellent books has explored, in great detail, how smart tech and Silicon Valley reflects dimensions of, to paraphrase bell hooks, a long-standing imperialist, ableist, patriarchal, heteronormative, white supremacist, capitalist regime.[6] An essential reading list includes, but is not limited to, *Dark Matters* (2015), *Digital Sociologies* (2016), *The Intersectional Internet* (2016), *Programmed Inequality* (2017), *Algorithms of Oppression* (2018), and *Automating Inequality* (2018).[7]

These injustices and harms do not have to be intentionally designed into the tech for them to have real effects on the world. If only that were the case, then the problem would be easily solved by weeding out malicious engineers or by adopting "Don't Be Evil" as a company-wide slogan, like Google did until even that gesture became too heavy of a burden.

Frequently, instead, they are the result of implicit biases, norms, and assumptions, which are then buried under layers of code. They are further spread by a culture that doesn't recognize how it reproduces inequity and exclusion, and doesn't have enough incentive to do things differently because the people who benefit from the status quo are the same people who make decisions about what to build and how to use it. As historian of technology Mar Hicks brilliantly writes in their research on early mainframe computers in 1950s' Britain,

> Yet, computing in the service of powerful interests, be they state or corporate, tends to inculcate stereotypes and static identities appropriate to reifying and perpetuating forms of existing power. The purpose of these systems is to discipline information in the service of a particular goal. In order to increase their own efficiency and power, such systems must stylize reality and translate it into an informational landscape where it can be acted upon in a seemingly frictionless, disinterested, and unbiased way. In point of fact, however, this

process of rendering information computable relies on institution-
alizing the views and biases of those constructing the system, and
reflexively serves their ends.[8]

Thus the rise of the digital age is not a disruptive break from
history. It is a new way of repackaging, reproducing, and revitalizing what came before. We have to look beyond the high-tech
veneer that covers up the machinations of old power regimes.[9]
The more things change, the more they stay the same.

Thesis Two

*Smart tech is a way of terraforming society for digital capitalism to
thrive.*

Terraforming is the idea of changing a planet's environment
so that it can support human life. In the next part, we will see
how smart tech is being used to remake primary places like work,
home, and the city. This version of terraforming, however, is
directed at creating conditions for a specific model of human life
that is engineered according to the imperatives of digital capitalism. In the process, it also changes how people live in and
interact with their environments.

Entrepreneurs talk about creating "ecosystems" of interconnected companies, platforms, apps, and devices. Independently,
each device or platform is just an insignificant addition to a stable environment, but as a whole the swarm takes over, disrupts
the equilibrium, and transforms the environment.

Yet we never hear about what kind of ecosystems are being
created. There are a variety of kinds. Is it a mutualistic ecosystem
based on cooperation and shared benefit? Is it symbiotic, where
the lives of different organisms are deeply interdependent? How
about a parasitic one with bloodsuckers draining the energy of

its host? Or perhaps it is the food chain hierarchy of predator versus prey. What matters is your place in the ecosystem, and whether you survive or thrive.

The new ecosystem is much more alien. It resembles a bio-dome where every aspect is continuously recorded and cyber-netically controlled. This is not just a divide between artificial and natural environments.[10] Rather, it is a transition toward creating increasingly micromanaged enclosures that record and react to the inhabitants' behaviors, while also regulating their behaviors.[11] It's the difference between the classic Honeywell thermostat that automatically keeps the room at a comfortable temperature, and the new Nest thermostat that also keeps track of data about who is at home, where they are located, and what their preferences are, and then reports that data to third parties in sectors such as insurance, energy, and security.[12]

As our workplaces, homes, and cities are turned into program-mable enclosures, the conditions are adjusted to create a desired equilibrium state that is conducive to the overgrowth of digital capitalism. Remember that the global corporation IBM, which specializes in selling large-scale systems and visions, calls this process "building a smarter planet."[13] This sure sounds like terra-forming by another name.

The same institutions seeking to create a smarter planet will also be its apex predator, well fed and secure. While some people won't reach the top of the food chain, they will have the resources and skills to adapt to the climatic changes of a planet built by/for digital capitalism. But large swaths of people will either be excluded from or enclosed by the smart planet; they will have to learn to survive and prove their worth in some way—or else be consumed. This future is not inevitable, nor has it fully come to pass, but it is the one we are currently hurtling toward.

Thesis Three

It is a privilege to not have access to many types of smart tech, to not use and be used by them, to be blissfully unaware of their existence.

Access to high-tech goods is usually seen as a privilege enjoyed by certain strata of society: the upper class with income to spare, the young urban professionals who want every advantage, or the tech-savvy geeks who camp out for the latest gadgets. While this might hold true for luxury upgrades, the cliché wears thin on closer inspection, especially when we consider more than just the phones in our pockets. There are plenty of cutting-edge applications of smart tech that the yuppies and geeks likely know nothing about.

Rather than the fitness wristband or virtual assistant, when we think about smart tech, we should instead think about the tracking devices installed in cars that enable lenders to shut off the engine if the driver misses a payment or the handheld scanner that enables employers to dictate every second of a worker's day. Or the scoring algorithm that enables data brokers to decide who can rent a home or get a job. Or the networked home appliance that enables insurers to optimize premiums and modify behavior, or the surveillance system that enables police to fix a persistent, penetrating gaze on the city.

Most important, in addition to thinking about tech, we should focus on the people whose interests it advances as well as the people who feel its impacts.

The outcomes of smart tech are not evenly distributed. The harms are disproportionately felt by the poor and people of color. At times, they are overrepresented by smart tech, such as when their lives are put under the microscope by government agencies and financial institutions, whereas privileged groups don't have to endure such close scrutiny just to access basic goods and services. At other times, they are missing or misrepresented in the data sets used to train software, such as when an artificial-intelligence-powered hiring tool systematically valued applications from men over women.[14] It's no coincidence that these programmed inequalities are common in a profession that is mostly male, white, and affluent.[15]

The marginalized are made to live in a parallel reality where they simultaneously experience the harms of inclusion in some systems and exclusion from others—where they cannot access some devices and are forced to use others—without necessarily receiving the benefits. Meanwhile, the privileged are largely unaware of this reality. For them, it's all convenience and connection—or for the most privileged class, power and profit—with hardly any of the material consequences.

Thesis Four

Common practices of data collection should be seen as theft and/or exploitation.

It is the strangely conspiratorial truth of the surveillance society we inhabit that there are unknown entities gathering our data for unknown purposes. Much of the valuable data harvested from the world is about people: our identities, beliefs, behaviors, and other personal information. This means collecting data often goes hand in hand with increasingly invasive systems for probing, tracking, and analyzing people.[16] Meeting demands for data extraction leads to the intensification of existing practices and creation of new ones.

Following in the footsteps of other extractive enterprises through capitalism's history, such as land grabs and resource mining, data is taken with little regard for *meaningful consent* and *fair compensation* for the people who that data is about.[17]

The issue of consent is relatively straightforward. Silicon Valley's near-total disregard for user consent has been made obvious by journalistic reporting, academic scholarship, and congressional inquiries. If companies seek consent to record, use, and/or sell a person's data, it is typically done in the form of a contract. The most common kind is called an end user license agreement (EULA). These are the pages on websites and mobile apps that make you click "agree" or "accept" before you can use the service. They are a hallmark of digital technology and account for, according to law professor Eyal Zamir, "more than 99% of the contracts currently entered."[18] As the world becomes smarter, these kinds of contracts are being smuggled into everything from cat litter boxes to vehicles.

EULAs are known as "boilerplate" contracts because they are generically applied to all users. They are one-sided, nonnegotiated, and nonnegotiable. They are long, dense legal documents, designed not to be read. You either unquestioningly agree or you are denied access. "It is hard, therefore, to consider them to be free and voluntary arrangements since one party has no power to enact their demands," explains political economist Kean Birch.[19] These companies don't seek consent; they demand compliance. This is far from the standard of informed, active consent that actually preserves our choice and autonomy.

The issue of compensation is more complicated, in large part because it can be difficult to put a fair price on personal information. Different types of data are valued differently by different businesses. Not all data can be, or is meant to be, converted into money. The value of data also rises nonlinearly as more data is collected. One individual's data may not be worth much, but the aggregated data of hundreds, thousands, or millions of individuals can be immensely valuable.[20] We can judge the fairness of compensation, however, by asking, What kind of compensation, if any, is offered for data, and how much is offered compared to the value obtained by data extractors?

Compensation most often comes in the form of access to services like Facebook's platform and Google's search engine. Rather than charging money to use the service, the owner collects data as payment. Even if we concede that many users think this is perfectly fair compensation, these service providers are outnumbered by the countless companies that collect, use, and sell personal data, typically without the knowledge of—let alone compensation for—the people whose data they capture.[21] Thus many data extractors fail the first test right away; receiving nothing can hardly be seen as fair.

The companies that offer services in exchange for our data and attention do provide us with some handy apps and platforms, although they also happen to be plagued with problems ranging from massive security breaches to election tampering. And what's their payment in return for these services? Lording over the new gilded age by hoarding the wealth and power of a multibillion-dollar (or trillion?) data economy.[22] This seems like a wildly unfair trade. Or at the very least, the fairness is up for serious debate and cannot just be assumed as given.

The common belief is that people—especially millennials who grew up with digital technology—no longer care about privacy. They are comfortable with giving up privacy for convenience. So-called thought leaders point to this supposed shift in attitudes to justify business models based on putting people under constant, invasive surveillance. Yet when you actually ask people what they think, you get a much more somber view.

In a survey of 1,106 people and interviews with randomly selected participants, media studies scholar Mark Andrejevic asked questions about their thoughts toward data collection and privacy. What he found is that people were not indifferent to privacy concerns but instead frequently expressed feelings of being "powerless" to do anything about data collection. As one participant said, "My biggest thing from loss of privacy isn't about other people knowing information about you but kind of being forced or bribed to share your information." That sense of powerlessness is intensified by a lack of knowledge about when, how, or why data collection happens, and what the consequences might even be. Another participant noted, "We really don't know where things collected about us go—we don't understand how they interact in such a complex environment."[23]

It's not that people don't care about privacy and data collection. Rather, they are denied the opportunities to do anything about it. In the face of relentless extraction, apathy is a defense mechanism.

When a thing is taken without consent, we call it *theft*. When people do not receive fair payment for a thing they have sold or labor they have done, we call it *exploitation*. It should not matter, ethically and legally speaking, if we're talking about digital personal information, as opposed to a material object or physical work.

No matter how high tech their methods and how polished their public image, the enterprises at the heart of digital capitalism are extractive. They recognize the value of data, and take advantage of political and legal systems that protect their rights to property and profit over our rights to consent and compensation. We should be eliminating corporate thievery, not tolerating yet another type.

Thesis Five

Datafication is violence.

First some definitions. Data is a recorded digital abstraction of something or somebody. Datafication is the process of making data by reducing and turning things into data. Abstraction is the process of simplifying a thing by stripping it of context and focusing only on specific qualities. All abstractions are only representations or simulations of a thing, not the thing itself.

Contrary to what you might have heard from people arguing online, neither data (the object) nor datafication (the process) grants us unmediated access to truth by somehow revealing the world as it really exists. These abstractions are much more powerful: they *order* and *construct* the world.[24] We know the cliché "knowledge is power," but we miss the other side of this relationship: power has an interest in deciding what counts as knowledge, how it spreads, who has it, and why it's used.[25] Datafication is a way to probe the world's features and dynamics, sort it into categories and norms, render it legible and observable, and exclude other metrics and methods of knowing it. Datafication is, like all ways of scrutinizing and sorting the world, also a way of exercising power over the world.[26]

When directed at people, datafication can be dehumanizing: it reduces people to abstractions about their attributes and associations, which are atomized, accumulated, analyzed, and administered. It turns humans into a form that can fit into sensors, servers, and processors. It enables smart systems in various sectors of society to profile, sort, stratify, score, rank, reward, punish, include, exclude, and otherwise calculate decisions that determine what sociologists call our "life-chances": the opportunities, pathways, and choices that are open to each of us.[27]

Not all these processes and outcomes are harmful; depending on who you are, many are beneficial or neutral, and most are normal. But that says more about the way society has been organized around data-driven systems rather than anything about the morality of datafication and abstraction. It shows how we have come to accept the existence of a vast machinery made to crunch humans into numbers.

The language that critical scholars and practitioners use to discuss datafication—data grabbing, data colonialism, data extraction—is a lexicon of violence. Instead of dancing around this relationship, we ought to be clear and explicit about the violence involved in abstracting human life, identity, and action. Not all violence is equally severe, but it is nonetheless still violence.

Our understanding of violence tends to be so parochial, with its focus on direct physical force, that it is almost hard to imagine violence on the scale that can be—and indeed, has been—carried out through datafication. Datafication is abstraction, but its results are not always abstract.

We can point to truly horrible examples like IBM selling punch card technology to the Nazis, thereby facilitating their ability to create and categorize detailed census records that were used to systematically carry out genocide.[28] But we don't need to evoke Godwin's law to find ordinary cases of what Anna Lauren Hoffmann has called "data violence."[29] We only need to look around and listen to the experiences of vulnerable and marginalized communities.[30] I mean hell, even the most advantaged among us have faced the frustration of glitches and mix-ups in the bureaucratic systems that administer our lives. Now imagine if a mistake in how data was collected or calculated was the difference between being arrested or not, receiving assistance or not, and many other algorithmic decisions that directly affect people every day.

In reality, there is often no "mistake" involved, but rather the outcomes of intentional choices and implicit biases. That's the violence of datafication.

Thesis Six

Platforms are the new landlords of digital capitalism.

Digital platforms—a stable of major ones includes Uber, Airbnb, Facebook, Google, Amazon, and many others—are now a form of critical infrastructure in society. They mediate our everyday activities. We build much of our social interactions, economic transactions, and personal consumption on top of these privately owned platforms. With the growing centrality and power of these platforms also comes the rapid expansion of rent extraction in contemporary society.[31]

Digital platforms insert themselves into any space they can—especially spaces that were previously nonmonetized—in a mission to skim value from every ad served, post shared, or thing sold. Their main strategy is to enclose everything we do, want, and need by turning them into "services" that take place on their platform. Uber offers "transportation-as-a-service." WeWork offers "space-as-a-service." Amazon Mechanical Turk offers "humans-as-a-service."[32] In addition to consumer services, many governments, businesses, universities, and other organizations now rent core services, such as software and storage, from platforms. These software-as-a-service operations take place within the ecosystem of private platforms, thus supplying those platforms with a continual source of revenue, while also solidifying their critical position in the economy and society.

The platform business model is based on two main features: applying pricing models based on pay as you go, subscriptions, and licensing to more things; and expanding the notion of rental payment to include not just dollars but also data. Ideally, for these landlords of digital capitalism, nobody would actually own anything. They would just rent it from a monopoly provider—until they can't afford the payments.

At the core of digital capitalism and the platform economy is what I call extraction-as-a-service. The aim is to develop innovative ways to make rent extraction as frictionless, automatic, and maximized as possible.

Unlike traditional landlords who demand payment from the use of real estate, the new rentiers capture revenue from the use of digital platforms. Crucially, they charge for access—not for ownership, which increasingly is framed as outdated. Platform companies, of course, do not call themselves landlords because doing so would be disastrous for their public image and reveal too much about how they operate. They instead use seductive language like "sharing" and make claims about "connecting people together." But the surge of business models that describe themselves as "Uber for X" or "X-as-a-service" are creating rentier relations by another name. In other words, what these companies are doing is actually revitalizing of an old form of rentier capitalism that we tend to associate with landlords and feudalism.

One of the key technologies of enclosure is the software license, which allows the companies to claim ownership over the software embedded in and data emanating from increasingly more objects that we use in our daily lives. With smart devices, the physical thing is bought, but the digital software is "licensed," which is just another word for "rented," and the constant stream of data we produce by using the thing constitutes part of the "rent" we pay to the company. By making what were once ordinary objects into smart things, companies are able to enact a form of microenclosure in which they retain ownership over the digital part of a physical thing—and the right to access, control, and shut off the software—even after you purchase it. With smart tech and digital capitalism, we have entered the age of the landlord 2.0.

If we take the logic of digital capitalism to its conclusion, the ultimate goal is to enact a radical shift: rather than being owners of anything, we become renters of everything at the mercy of licensing agreements that render us powerless. The contracts sap us of any efficacy for determining the rules of the digital world we live in. They enforce a one-sided power that benefits the corporations that draw up the contractual terms. We are expected to submit to their unjust, unfair procedures without question, as if there were no other possible ownership regimes. Whether we are streaming content or licensing software, we are paying for the privilege of slowly ceding control of private property to corporate gatekeepers.

It's one thing for digital controls to restrict how you can use a smart cat litter box. But it seems another thing to spend $30,000 buying a car, or even $100,000 on a tractor, if all you own is a big hunk of metal and rubber while only renting the software needed to actually operate the vehicle. While contracts like terms of services grew out of software and websites, they are now used as a way for digital platforms to smuggle ownership claims into parts of things that are otherwise owned by somebody else.

Now instead of building fences and demanding rent for access to landed property, these rentiers install software and capture value from the use of digital platforms and physical things.

If this movement of landlords 2.0 had a motto, it would be this: Why limit rent collection to real estate when there is a whole world out there waiting to capture rent from, online and off?

Thesis Seven

The Great Recession might be renamed the Great Disruption.

Data is often called the "new oil" because it fuels the systems that have made society smart and generates massive wealth for a fast-growing industry. The cover of a 2017 issue of the *Economist* proclaimed "The World's Most Valuable Resource" over an illustration of offshore oil platforms labeled with the names of major digital platforms like Facebook, Google, and Uber that are drilling for data.[33] Rather than simply laugh off these metaphors as trite clichés, we should take a cue from them and treat big data with the same wariness we direct toward big oil and big finance. These are, after all, industries driven by the same reckless desire for profit and power that has shaped the world at every level—socially, politically, economically, and environmentally—perhaps irreversibly.

In 2010, journalist Matt Taibbi described Goldman Sachs as a "great vampire squid wrapped around the face of humanity, relentlessly jamming its blood funnel into anything that smells like money."[34] At the time, many people were largely unaware that Silicon Valley was busy laying the groundwork for its own extractive enterprise. We were focused on the parasitic and criminal activities of Wall Street. In contrast to the old robber barons in dark suits, the brash young guns in hoodies looked harmless. Perhaps they'll even live up to their lofty promises of *making the world a better place.*

Yet beneath this clever branding was a voracious hunger for the personal data that we all undervalued. They took advantage of favorable public opinion and shiny gadgets to ensnare us with tech designed to be addictive, normalize invasive surveillance of our private lives, and hoard ungodly amounts of wealth. In recent years, people have realized that these techno-oligarchs and digital capitalists aren't actually making the word better. But that realization only came after another vampire squid has latched onto our face.

The relationship between Wall Street and Silicon Valley is closer than we often think. It's no coincidence that some of the largest platforms—Uber, Airbnb, and WeWork—were founded a decade ago in the immediate aftermath of the global financial crash. With finance marked by toxic assets, there was plenty of capital looking for other places to invest. Whereas other industries and governments were shaken to their core, the postcrash landscape created the conditions for tech companies selling smart solutions and digital platforms to thrive. In no time, they grew to be significant features of cities around the world.

Long-term recession and unrelenting austerity measures have meant that many cities in the West are struggling with outdated, inadequate infrastructure and underfunded, overcapacity agencies. A shrinking public sector and struggling economy has opened up the market to new platforms that want to take control of services that are central to life for billions of people: how we travel, get food, rent rooms, find workspace, and do just about everything.

For the venture capitalists and ambitious entrepreneurs in Silicon Valley, their strategy for world domination relies on changing regulation, driving out competition, gaining monopoly power, and controlling essential services in society.[35] In a paper on "regulatory entrepreneurship," law professors Elizabeth Pollman and Jordan Barry explain that this practice "is not new, but it has become increasingly salient in recent years as companies from Airbnb to Tesla, and from DraftKings to Uber, have become agents of legal change."[36]

Unlike local governments with barely a penny to spare, tech companies have massive reserves of capital to burn. They can seduce cities with promises of innovation while sustaining a campaign of disruption against holdouts. For instance, Uber has openly said it wants to focus on expanding into new areas like mass transit by introducing services such as UberHop that effectively compete with buses. It's easy to imagine Uber's notoriously ruthless lobbyists shaking down cities, basically saying, "That's a nice public transportation system you have there; it would be a shame if something happened to it."

Now take this threat and apply it to potentially every part of daily life, function of a city, and element of government. In effect, these tech companies aim to acquire what Frank Pasquale calls functional sovereignty: "From room-letting to transportation to commerce, persons will be increasingly subject to corporate, rather than democratic, control."[37] No longer content with reigning over cyberspace, tech companies have realized what property developers knew all along: city space is where the real action's at.

As ground zero for the financial crash, much critical attention has been focused on Wall Street. But in the grand scheme, Silicon Valley's ascension as corporate sovereign could be one of the crash's most important consequences.

Thesis Eight

The most insidious product of Silicon Valley is not a technology but rather an ideology.

The language of Silicon Valley—filled with vapid buzzwords and naive sentiments—is almost beyond parody. It's easy to forget that words actually have meaning and utility. Even more, that this way of talking about the world has spread far beyond Silicon Valley to other halls of power. "These aren't harmless verbal frames," explains media theorist Ian Bogost. "They are signs of our willingness to allow a certain kind of technological thinking to take over all other thinking."[38] This way of thinking, with its set of ideas, beliefs, values, and goals, is a contemporary update to an ideology called technocracy.

At the core of the technocratic ideology is a deeply held "solutionism": the belief that all the world's problems, even those that should not be thought of as problems in the first place, can be solved technologically.[39] By recasting everything as a problem waiting for a technofix, the space for philosophical reflection and political debate shrinks, particularly when applied to problems that are fundamentally social in nature.

The solutionist ideology works backward: those in the business of selling solutions need solvable problems, and thus every problem is framed in a way that justifies the solutions that are readily available, fit a certain frame of the world, and/or most benefit the seller. Invention becomes the mother of necessity.

Wherever they are found, whatever shape they take, technocrats attempt to legitimize their power over others by offering innovative proposals they claim are untainted by troubling subjective biases and interests. Through rhetorical appeals to optimization and objectivity, technocrats depict their solutions to society's problems as pragmatic alternatives to inefficient political procedures.[40]

Technocracy can be thought of as a kindred spirit to authoritarianism, which disregards democratic decision making and moral complexity in favor of rule by experts who can engineer the path to utopia.[41] For technocrats, all human values can be ignored, downplayed, or recast as technical parameters. Any trade-offs and assumptions are hidden inside simplistic cost-benefit analysis. There are no valid disagreements to be had, only obvious decisions to be made. The question is never "why" do something, but "how" to do it. They do things not because they should but instead because they can.

The technocratic mind-set—this ideology of the supposedly nonideological—will sound familiar to anybody who has heard a keynote by the entrepreneurs, engineers, and executives who find a welcome home in Silicon Valley. This ranges from Elon Musk's disgust at the idea of riding public transportation (solution: underground tunnels) to investor Marc Andreessen's anger at India for blocking Facebook's expansion into a new market (solution: embrace colonialism).[42] Not surprisingly, the modern technocrat tends to focus on problems and solutions that concern their idiosyncratic desires and dislikes, or improves their net worth and influence, all while making claims about "saving the world."

Fundamentally, technocrats believe they possess a toolbox that can be universally applied to solve all problems. With this belief comes a deep arrogance about their own ability, deep disregard about other approaches, and deep naivete about their own limitations.

We are promised a futuristic society that is engineered to run like a hyperefficient machine. All we have to do is hand over control to tech corporations and trust in the benevolence of capitalism with Silicon Valley characteristics.

Thesis Nine

Like other political projects, building the smart society is a battle for our imagination.

Telling stories about the future is a way of shaping the present. If you can direct and delimit what people can imagine as possible, then you can set the parameters for what kind of society we live in. Former UK prime minister Margaret Thatcher knew this when she famously declared, regarding the economic program of neoliberalism, "There is no alternative." The imagineers and thought leaders in Silicon Valley know this too when they describe technology as a deterministic, inhuman force that only advances in one direction, marching toward progress. "Like a force of nature, the digital age cannot be denied or stopped," declared Nicholas Negroponte, the founder of the MIT Media Lab.[43] This is the tech entrepreneur's way of announcing that the end of history has arrived, carried on the wings of ubiquitous computing and internet connections. What threat could there be from people who cannot even imagine a different way of life?

The tech sector is a prime case study in how grabbing hold of our collective imagination is one of the most effective tactics for gaining and maintaining power.[44] Building a smart society involves much more than just engineering algorithms, devices, and platforms. It also requires selling a vision of the future and plotting a road map for how to get there.[45] That road map might not actually lead us to the promised destination—it might well be filled with dead-ends and detours—but that matters less than the ability to convince people that there is no other feasible pathway forward.

While tech companies claim to be fiercely innovative and disruptive, driven by a desire to change the world, they never actually sketch a range of alternative futures. They eschew truly radical visions that might challenge the status quo or their position. Instead, they offer a curated selection of solutions and scenarios with the aim of establishing their version of a smart society as *the future*—the only one available or possible.

At its base, politics is a contest to see whose plan for governing society is made into reality. For all their talk of technology being outside politics, ultimately the strategists in Silicon Valley know what's at stake and intend to be the winners of this technopolitical battle.

As the well-known phrase goes, "It is easier to imagine the end of the world than to imagine the end of capitalism."[46] Capitalism's place in society is so pervasive that it has even inhibited the most radical, creative thinkers alive from conceiving of a different world. We are steeped in capitalism. It has saturated the fabric of society and fiber of our being. It is a dynamic system that adapts over time to sociotechnical changes—in large part by controlling those changes—and absorbs everything into its processes.

Capitalism's invasiveness and stickiness cannot be chalked up to a conspiracy theory—though, it might feel like that sometimes. Its influence over our imaginations is not due to techniques for brainwashing the masses, like chemtrails in the sky. The process at work is less exciting and less complex than the tales of shadowy cabals ruling over us.

The real conspiracy here is one of class domination. This is an old story about power and ideology, the maintenance of influence by those at the top, and the promotion of certain interests over others. It results in a regime of governance built on gross inequality and oligarchic rule. "A structure where one man gets to decide whether hundreds of thousands of people will be able to feed their children or pay rent is intolerable," writes journalist Alex Press about Jeff Bezos's decision to raise Amazon's minimum wage to fifteen dollars per hour.[47] Capitalism—in any variety, digital or otherwise—is a system that is both intolerable and enduring, but not inevitable.

Conspiracy theory offers a cheap way out of engaging with politics: if only we could uncover the secret machinations and damning evidence, then everybody will realize what's really going and the world will be fixed! Political theory does not offer "one weird trick" for achieving a better world but rather provides something even better: it allows us to see that society is governed by people, and the things/choices they make are contingent. This means—contrary to the cries of "no alternative"—that different people can make different decisions and build different things based on different values and for different purposes. There is hope in this realization, and that should motivate action.

We cannot forget that the version of a smart society outlined in this book is still a future in the making. We must not mistake a fallible plan for an inevitable fate. The fight for our imagination—and the world it gives shape to—is not yet over.

Thesis Ten

Silicon Valley has until now tried to control the world in various ways; the point is to liberate it.

Resistance to digital capitalism cannot be achieved through quick fixes and individual choices. No digital detox, in which you abstain from looking at screens and hooking into the internet, is going to combat a political economic system fueled by squeezing value from data and attention. No mindfulness app, which reminds you to take a few moments to sit quietly every day, is going to steel you against a political economic system designed to concentrate power in the hands of a few. These things might help us tolerate the worst excesses of digital capitalism—to be sure, every little bit of relief helps—but they aren't going to change the system. Ensuring everybody enjoys the benefits of and has representation within a technological society requires collective action.

The last chapter explains three tactics for working toward a better world. But before that, let's get a better understanding of the smart society as it currently exists.

II Machinery of a Smart Society

5 Pretty Rate Machine

> He sits motionless, like a spider in the center of its web, but that web has a thousand radiations, and he knows well every quiver of each of them.
>
> —Sherlock Holmes, describing the criminal mastermind Moriarty in *The Memoirs of Sherlock Holmes*, 1894/2010

Candice Smith was driving on the freeway in Las Vegas, Nevada, when "all of a sudden the steering wheel locks up," reported the *New York Times*.[1] Her car shut off and careened across multiple lanes of traffic. Thanks to a stroke of luck and help from fellow drivers, Candice managed to stop the car without seriously hurting anybody.

Mary Bolender's daughter had a dangerously high fever of 103.5 degrees. She knew her sick kid needed to get to the emergency room right away. They rushed to her van. She turned the key. It wouldn't start. She tried again, but the vehicle was dead, as if the engine had been removed. Mary, a single mother, "felt absolutely helpless."[2]

Michelle Fahy picked up her four children from school, and on the way home, stopped at a gas station to fill up her car. After pumping fuel, she tried to restart the car. Nothing happened.

She pleaded for her car to come back to life, but it just sat there, immobile and useless. The longer they were stranded, the more confused and worried her children became. "They were in panic mode," Michelle said.[3]

On what was surely one of the most stressful days of their lives, all three women were victims of remote repossession.

Not long ago, the repo man would show up in the middle of the night and tow away the vehicles of people who missed their car payments. But now repo men don't have use the cover of night to "legally steal vehicles," as repossession has been called. They can ride shotgun—always taking note of where you are, and always able to take away your car—in the form of a smart device installed in vehicles.

The "starter interrupt device" allows auto lenders to track the location of cars, both in real time and over time, and remotely shut off vehicles if the borrower falls behind on payments (sometimes by only a day) or drives outside an approved area. There's no escaping debt collectors who can, with the push of a button on their smartphones, disable your car until you cough up payment. As one lender said, "I have disabled a car while I was shopping at Walmart."[4] No effort, no stealth, no confrontation required.

The three examples above are from a recent investigation by the *New York Times* into the growing use of starter interrupt devices by auto lenders.[5] While these stories are particularly harrowing, they are not uncommon. It is routine for many lenders who lease cars to subprime borrowers to require the installation of starter interrupt devices in vehicles. We tend to associate "subprime" with mortgages and the toxic assets that contributed to the 2008 financial crash. Subprime loans, however, are not just for homes. A 2016 study shows that almost half of all auto loans in the United States are going to borrowers labeled "subprime," which means they have poor credit scores and are considered financially risky.[6] PassTime, a leading manufacturer of starter interrupt devices, has sold millions of them to auto lenders, car dealers, and insurance companies around the world. Indeed, the business magazine *Inc.* named PassTime one of "America's fastest-growing private companies" in 2015.[7]

These lenders claim they would not extend credit to subprime borrowers if it weren't for the starter interrupt device. They frame this technology of control as a form of "tough love" meant to help people "get on their feet" and stay on the right track.[8] They also cast the device as a necessary trade-off that people—usually poor and/or of color—must make if they want the privilege of mobility.

But don't let the supposed goodwill of auto lenders fool you. The devices are meant to amplify their ability to extract payment by expanding their power over spaces, objects, and people. In addition to GPS tracking and remote repo, one type of device beeps every five seconds on the day your payment is due. That's the kind of aggressively tough love that nobody deserves to endure. The device's origins speak volumes about the power dynamics built into it; an early version was used to help pet owners keep track of their animals.

As plenty of research shows, especially after the 2008 financial crash, the techniques used by subprime lenders are less about extending credit to risky people than they are about maximizing profit margins.[9] The starter interrupt device is an extreme example of how disadvantaged people are now exploited in new ways. Lenders cynically use the language of fairness and opportunity to justify a system that strips away privacy, autonomy, and dignity. What's more, the danger that the starter interrupter poses to borrowers, and other drivers who share the road with a vehicle that might shut off while moving or idling, is problematic in its own right.

And yet these devices are not aberrations. The starter interrupt device is simply a more in-your-face example of the myriad ways in which smart tech is used to monitor and manage people. Everything from the location tracking and remote control to value extraction and behavioral modification is straight out of the digital capitalism handbook. The device's use by predatory lenders heightens our reaction to its features and impacts, but we should also be careful not to treat it as an isolated case of smart tech gone awry.

Virginia Eubanks, a scholar of technology and justice, points out that a good way to predict the future of data collection and social control is to ask poor and marginalized groups since they are typically the "test subjects for surveillance technologies." As one woman on welfare told Eubanks, "You should pay attention to what happens to us. You're next."[10] By this she meant white, middle-class professionals like Eubanks (and myself).

When it's not being tested and trained on vulnerable communities, smart tech might first appear as high-end consumer goods on the market, where they are used by early adopters and people with disposable incomes. In both cases, if the tech is effective and lucrative, then the smart features are integrated into products as standard. Gradually the tech is rolled out to the rest of us and spreads throughout society until it becomes a normal part of life. This is what happened with many early developments in electronics and digital computing.

For instance, the insurance company Progressive gives customers a device called Snapshot to install in their cars. The device records where, when, and how you drive, and then streams that information back to Progressive. Do you "hard brake" too often? Do you speed, even when nobody is around? Do you drive through "dangerous" neighborhoods? Do you drive at odd hours? Well now your policy premium can accurately reflect these factors. As the company's CEO said, Snapshot is a "meaningful start toward personalized insurance pricing based on real-time measurement of your driving behavior—the statistics of one."[11]

While Snapshot won't be used to disable a driver's ignition, it does help Progressive monitor and manage drivers in other ways. Many other insurers are now using similar devices, such as Little-Box, which the UK insurer Admiral offers customers as part of its Black Box Insurance program. If insurers don't want to develop this smart tech in-house, they can hire the services offered by start-ups like the Floow, which collects data from the sensors in a driver's smartphone and analyzes that data to assign each driver a "safety score." The start-up then predicts how likely they are to have an accident in the near future. The Floow's analysis will then directly affect the driver's insurance premium.

Think of these devices and analytics as the middle-class version of the starter interrupt device. Those with the privilege to avoid hard control by auto lenders are coaxed into submitting to soft control by auto insurers.[12]

We are already subjected to a wide range of systems designed in various ways to collect our data and control our behaviors. We don't have to rely on radical examples. Nor do we need to predict the future to see how smart tech is shaping who we are, what we can do, and how we are judged. The *smart self* is already here.

Those familiar with a hot topic like self-tracking might expect a chapter on the "smart self" to focus on things like the

Quantified Self movement, the latest trends in wearable devices, and the history of bodily measurement. Without a doubt, these topics are interesting and important parts of the smart self. Yet they have also already attracted plenty of attention from adept researchers and journalists.[13] I want to argue instead that the smart self involves much more than just how people choose to track themselves. By looking at two cases of smart tech in action, scoring systems and managing workers, we will see that the major impacts of the smart self arise from what powerful people and institutions do with your data, and how they direct your behavior—whether you want them to or not.

Scoring Systems: Or, Wheeling and Dealing Data

It is the strangely conspiratorial truth of the surveillance society we inhabit that there are unknown entities gathering our data for unknown purposes. Companies and governments dip into the data streams of our lives in increasingly innovative ways, harvesting information on what we do, who we know, and where we go. The methods and purposes of data collection keep expanding, with seemingly no end or limit in sight.

A massive industry has been built on systems that aggregate thousands of data points about each individual person. These companies, called data brokers, capture our personal information and categorize us according to various metrics. The profiles they create are like virtual avatars: the data doubles of a dividualized self. By selling access to our data and profiles to other businesses—like marketers, insurers, and employers as well as government agencies and police departments—judgments made based on our virtual avatars directly affect our actual opportunities and welfare.

Data brokers are estimated to generate around $200 billion in annual revenue.[14] The three largest data brokers alone—Experian, Equifax, and TransUnion—each bring in billions of dollars annually. The size of these data banks is striking. According to a 2014 report by the US Federal Trade Commission, which investigated nine of the largest data brokers,

> One data broker's database has information on 1.4 billion consumer transactions and over 700 billion aggregated data elements; another data broker's database covers one trillion dollars in consumer transactions; and yet another data broker adds three billion new records each month to its databases. Most importantly, data brokers hold a vast array of information on individual consumers. For example, one of the nine data brokers has 3000 data segments for nearly every U.S. consumer.[15]

Data brokers tend to work from the shadows, but the industry was thrown into the public spotlight in September 2017 when Equifax was hacked, exposing the personal information of 143 million people.[16] The data accessed by hackers contained extremely sensitive information like social security, driver's license, and credit card numbers. Yet as monumental as Equifax's hack was, it only represented a fraction of the reserves hoarded by data brokers. Experian and TransUnion are data giants on par with Equifax, and there are thousands of other data brokers that are only small by comparison, not to mention all the massive databases held by companies that are supposedly not cutting deals to sell our data to third parties.

Data brokers use all this information to slice society into market segments. An investigation into the industry's operations revealed that the categories it uses can be callous and even ghoulish. For example, some categories include "fragile families," "gullible elderly," "probably bipolar," "rape victim," and "daughter killed in a car crash."[17] In the mission to squeeze value from data, everything is fair game if it boosts the industry's ability to target and exploit people.

Data brokers also sort us by using less macabre categories like demographics, consumer choices, and political views. If that data is not readily apparent, then brokers claim they can use other information to infer our identities and predict our preferences. For instance, if you live in a certain postal code, work at a fast-food joint, and don't own a car, then the data broker can use analytics—or stereotypes dressed up as algorithmic analysis—to assume your race, age, education, and socioeconomic status. Even when data is supposedly anonymous, plenty of studies show that it is not too difficult for those with the rights tools and knowledge to figure out somebody's identity and other intimate details by using just a handful of data points about them.[18]

Information can then be merged from multiple databases to provide an even more complete profile of your identity and behavior—which can then be used in unexpected and unsettling ways. For example, some hospitals and health insurers have used data brokers to buy people's credit card purchase history. While you might be pleased to see that your insurer rewarded you for buying a gym membership (even if you rarely go anymore), you might also be surprised to see that your insurer decided to penalize you for buying McDonald's too often.[19] (I will dive deeper into the insurance industry's eager embrace of smart tech in the next chapter.) Thanks to data brokers, information that was siloed can now be fused and used in alarming new ways.

In addition to building profiles, many data brokers provide credit scoring services, so on top of categorizing us, they judge and rank us. The profiles and scores they create are then used to make choices that directly impact many facets of our lives, such as obtaining a loan, renting a home, or finding a job.[20] The "marketing scores" they assign to each person are carefully designed to evade regulations meant to rein in unjust uses of such data dossiers.[21] Legislation like the Fair Credit Reporting Act was intended to end the collection of "irrelevant" information and established rules for the "permissible" uses of consumer reports. But due to wily legal maneuvering, this law does not apply to data brokers.

There are effectively no restrictions on how data brokers assemble and sell their profiles, nor is there any oversight or transparency. These companies operate on opacity. Even a US Senate committee investigation into data brokers could not obtain substantial answers to the question of how brokers collect and use data.[22] It was stonewalled by a powerful industry that prizes its own privacy while profiting from invading everybody else's privacy. This leaves those of us who are profiled and scored—which means all of us—with no recourse. Even if the data brokers' profiles of you are totally wrong or incomplete, even if their scores are based on shoddy assumptions, it is difficult to correct the record. That is, if you even know about them. Meanwhile, these inaccurate assessments will still have real impacts.

These companies trade on the idea that their data-driven systems are objective and neutral. Their outputs are framed as accurate reflections of the world, thereby allowing them to escape blame for any harmful, unjust outcomes. They might say in response to challenges about their method of analysis, *Those are just the facts; it isn't our fault if you don't like the way the world works!* But in reality, these "weapons of math destruction," as computer scientist Cathy O'Neil calls them, smuggle in a host of stereotypes, biases, and errors.[23] They both reflect and reproduce long-standing inequalities.

"Just as neighborhoods can serve as a proxy for racial or ethnic identity, there are new worries that big data technologies could be used to 'digitally redline' unwanted groups, either as customers, employees, tenants, or recipients of credit," warns a 2014 report from the White House about big data's impacts.[24] The term "digital redline" conjures up the days when banks would draw a red line on a map around areas of the city—typically places where blacks, Latinxs, Asians, or other marginalized people lived—to denote places they would not lend money, at least not at fair rates. Data brokers take this stratification to the next level. Rather than overt discrimination, companies can rely on proxies for race, gender, and other "protected categories," and then draw correlations and conclusions that have discriminatory effects, while maintaining enough plausible deniability to avoid regulatory pushback.

As legal scholars have shown, the techniques used by data brokers played a critical but largely invisible role in the financial crash of 2008 by helping lenders find vulnerable people who could be lured into signing up for toxic subprime mortgages.[25] My own work with activist and author Astra Taylor has shown how targeted ads on Facebook, powered by personalized profiling, have been used by unscrupulous financial companies to trick and scam vulnerable people like single mothers and indebted students.[26] Since the crash, data brokers have not only evaded punishment but their capabilities for tracking and targeting people have become more sophisticated and lucrative too. "Now the system has exploded, where you've got all these actors that you don't actually have a relationship with: network advertisers, data brokers, companies that are vacuuming up information," according to Edmund Mierzwinski of the US Public Interest Research Group.[27]

We do not have to look hard to see other examples of how this data is used to fuel systems of exclusion and exploitation. Famously, cyberpunk pioneer William Gibson said that "the future is already here—it's just not evenly distributed."[28] If we want to see how these data-driven systems are developing, then we don't have to look into a crystal ball. We only need to look at a place that has taken the kind of systems developed in the United States and Europe, and run with them, while also refracting them through its own values and motivations: China.

The Leaderboard of Life

The mobile payment app Alipay is wildly popular in China. Developed by Ant Financial, an affiliate of e-commerce giant Alibaba—think of it as a fusion of Amazon, eBay, and PayPal, but with even more functions—Alipay is used by over five hundred million people for daily transactions. In many ways, Alipay is more like a bank combined with a large mobile ecosystem. People use it to buy groceries, pay bills, buy insurance, invest money, order dinner, call an Uber, book flights, and so much more. Indeed, Ant Financial has a potential valuation of $150 billon (as of early 2019), raising almost as much venture capital in 2018 as all US and European financial tech companies combined.[29] Alipay has built its reputation on being convenient and reliable—no hassles, no worries. Its slogan is "Trust makes it simple." One day in 2015, users of Alipay saw a new icon on the app's home screen for a service called Zhima Credit, which takes the idea of trust to a new level.

Zhima Credit (or Sesame Credit) analyzes the wealth of data collected by Alibaba about every user of Alipay—plus data acquired from partnerships with a long list of other companies—to assign each person a social credit score. This score is an assessment of your worth, reputation, and status wrapped up into a three-digit number. If you ever thought to yourself, "I wonder if I can trust this person?" well now you don't have to guess. Zhima Credit tells you.

Even though the scoring system was only launched a few years ago, it has rapidly spread through China. It is more than just a fun game or curious novelty. It has real influence over how individuals are treated by other people, businesses, and even government agencies. It echoes the FICO credit score that has been widely used in the United States for decades, but in the way that echoes sound instantly familiar yet distorted. This is due in large part to the fact that it leapfrogged the long course of development that credit scores took in the West, emerging in a society that is fully equipped with surveillance systems and connected lives.

Just as data brokers now integrate a wide variety of data into their profiles and scores, the Zhima Credit score is based on way more than just financial data. Cheating on a college entrance exam, neglecting to pay a traffic fine, having friends with low scores, playing video games too often, or posting negative things online about the Communist Party of China—all this could impact your credit score.[30] Alibaba keeps its "complex algorithm" secret, but it has revealed five broad factors it takes into account: credit histories, personal characteristics, interpersonal relationships, the fulfillment of contractual obligations, and behaviors and preferences.[31]

The score, ranging from 350 to 950, serves as a nationwide system that dictates your standing in society and how others treat you. High score? You are seen as an honest, respected citizen. Low score? You are labeled a swindler who is not to be trusted. People even display their score in dating apps as a way of attracting dates. The perks of having a high score also go beyond low interest rates; they include skipping the security line at airports and jumping the waiting list for health care. A low score, on the other hand, means being denied access to good job opportunities and foreign travel visas. For the digital underclass, even renting a bike requires a hefty deposit.

People work hard to raise their scores by buying the right things, interacting with the right people, and doing the right things. There are reputation consultants for hire and private chat rooms where high-score people swap tips. It's not so much gaming the system as it is becoming the type of person the system wants you to be. It is not a bug that people are scrambling to produce "positive data" that pleases the black-boxed algorithm but rather a feature of systems that hold power to rate, reward, and punish us.[32] This kind of disciplinary effect—in which people try to behave how they think the assessor wants them to behave—is designed into the operations of gatekeeping scores like Zhima Credit and FICO. When the disciplinary power fails and people step out of line, that's when the power of control comes into play through, for example, the use of blacklists that take away rights and privileges.

By 2020, the Chinese government plans to launch its Social Credit System (SCS) initiative. The SCS will be a mandatory, government-run version of Zhima Credit, built with the help of Baidu, one of the world's largest tech corporations. "The aim is for every Chinese citizen to be trailed by a file compiling data from public and private sources by 2020, and for those files to be searchable by fingerprints and other biometric characteristics," WIRED reports.[33] In mid-2018, the government announced it would begin instituting an early feature of the SCS: travel bans.

If people commit certain "social misdeeds," like failing to pay fines, they will be blacklisted from traveling on planes and trains for up to a year.[34]

The Chinese government is doing more than just watching and learning from the social credits scores operated by companies like Ant Financial; it is sharing much of the data these companies rely on. "Alibaba announced that less than 20 percent of the data used to assess personal credit come from Alibaba itself, and more than 80 percent of the data are collected from other sources, particularly government databases," notes Caixin, a Chinese business media outlet.[35] Once the SCS is fully launched, it will take over these other scores. The SCS is planned to be the ultimate, unified smart system. It aims to be more extensive, invasive, and consequential—composed of over four hundred data sets, five hundred variables, and fifty central government agencies.[36] According to a government policy document, the SCS's guiding principle is, "If trust is broken in one place, restrictions are imposed everywhere."[37]

For those in the West, it is easy to claim that Zhima Credit and the SCS are products of an authoritarian regime. It's tempting to sit back and say, "Wow, I'm glad I live in a free country where nothing like that would happen," or even worse, use these reports as evidence for why the United States or Europe is superior to China. But this shallow response completely misses the point. The logics and technologies at work in the social credit scores are not just some Orientalist dystopia dreamed up by the big bad Chinese. They are only somewhat amped up versions of what exists in the United States and Europe. If this is a dystopian dream, then it is shared and lucid.

It's unfortunately common that journalists and scholars can have the most critical, informed eye about surveillance and control in other places—particularly ones like China, where there is a long history of Cold War antagonism—while also unable to see the same kinds of systems existing all around them. We in the West already rate and rank everything—and in return, we are rated and ranked. We are assigned an untold number of scores created in hidden ways by secretive organizations and used for "unintended" purposes. For example, in September 2018 the Department of Homeland Security proposed using applicants' credit scores to help decide which immigrants get to live in the United States.[38]

The systems in China are not actually a crystal ball. They necessarily reflect the social and political context of China, and will look different in the United States or Europe, even if their processes lead to many of the same end points. What we should do is look at them as examples of how these smart systems can develop, and then consider how they are likely to continue advancing under a deeply stratified, totally surveilled, highly corporatized version of digital capitalism—you know, the kind that is being perfected by the United States and its allies.

Indeed, data brokers and government agencies in the United States and China likely covet aspects of each other's systems. Shazeda Ahmed, scholar of internet policy in China, writes that

> the current state of the social credit system is far less sophisticated than its portrayal in the foreign press. But if the scope of what can count as blacklist data widens, and if the tech sector takes an even more pervasive "searchlight" approach to seamlessly melding these data into their core offerings, the system could move much closer to the dystopian picture that appears in the media. In particular, if China embraces the marketization of blacklist data—so that data is bought and sold, like in the US—information about individuals would become even harder to track and contest.[39]

It's not hard to imagine an international integration of social scoring systems. Why should each country have its own credit score when a global system can be more holistic, complete, and powerful? Such a merger could finally actually give us the worst of both worlds.

Managing Workers: Or, In These Modern Times

The classic Charlie Chaplin film *Modern Times* (1936) is a brilliant satire of what the opening scene calls "a story of industry, of individual enterprise."[40] The film depicts the dehumanizing nature of industrial society, and shows how mechanical innovations were used to increase efficiency and maximize exploitation. Even though the film was made over eighty years ago, with just some simple updates to the job and tech, it could be about today.

The film starts with Chaplin as a hapless worker in a factory. We see various parts of his grueling workday. The boss oversees everybody by flipping through screens installed all around the factory. The screens are a two-way video: they not only allow the boss to monitor the whole factory from his office but also show the workers that the boss is watching. This type of surveillance might bring to mind George Orwell's novel *1984*, which was published thirteen years *after* Chaplin's film.

The scene then cuts to Chaplin, who is working on an assembly line. The speed of the machine often outpaces him, forcing him to work double time just to keep up. Soon Chaplin clocks out for a break and goes to the toilets, hoping to get a brief moment alone to rest. Shortly after catching his breath, a monitor in the toilets switches on and the boss yells at Chaplin, "Hey! Quit stalling and get back to work."

Soon the whistle blows for lunchtime. We see a group of inventors pitching a new laborsaving technology to the boss called the Billows Feeding Machine. They just need a guinea pig to demonstrate it in action; the boss chooses Chaplin. An engineer describes the machine as "a practical device which automatically feeds your men while at work. Don't stop for lunch, be ahead of your competitor. The Billows Feeding Machine will eliminate the lunch hour, increase your production, and decrease your overhead." Chaplin is strapped into the machine and force-fed while he works on the assembly line. The machine malfunctions, pummeling him with its mechanical arms and shoving food into his face.

Fast-forward to near the end of the workday. Chaplin is exhausted, but still working on the assembly line. In a desperate attempt to keep up with the rapid pace of the conveyor belt, Chaplin gets pulled into the giant machine. In one of the most famous scenes of the movie, Chaplin is seen getting crushed by massive gears that push him through the churning insides of the machine, as if he's being chewed and digested by a mechanical monster. All that's missing is a label on the machine that reads "industrial capitalism." His fellow workers throw the machine into reverse, and it spits Chaplin back out. Battered and fatigued, Chaplin suffers a nervous breakdown, and the boss has the police haul him off to the hospital—another casualty of capitalism.

Modern Times ingeniously skewered work and life in industrial society. Even today it remains a masterful film, but what if we made a sequel called *Contemporary Times* about work in a smart society? What would it look like? Instead of a factory in the 1930s, perhaps it would be set in the early twenty-first century's version of a brutally exploitative work place: an Amazon warehouse.

Work Smarter—and Harder

It is the first day on the job at the warehouse—Amazon calls them "fulfillment centers"—which just recently opened about an hour outside the city.[41] The cohort of new hires arrives before dawn for training day.[42] Most of these people have been hit hard by a stagnant economy and bleak job market. They are desperate for a paycheck. Amazon knows it has significant leverage over the army of temporary workers it relies on.[43] Perhaps these rookies have heard the same piece of advice told to Mac McClelland, a journalist who worked in a warehouse, by a staff member at the local chamber of commerce: "They hire and fire constantly, every day. You'll see people dropping all around you. But don't take it personally and break down or start crying when they yell at you."[44]

The warehouse is a colossal, cavernous, concrete structure. Inside are multiple floors filled with endless rows of shelves. Conveyor belts cut through the warehouse carrying boxes to different stations. If you work in one of the warehouses outfitted with Kiva robotics, then a section of the warehouse will be a "human exclusion zone," where a swarm of robotic platforms move shelves around in a networked choreography. This zone is dark, quiet, and off-limits. Any human who gets in the way could be seriously injured, and perhaps more importantly for Amazon's bottom line, disrupt the system's careful coordination. Descriptions of the human exclusion zones have a Lovecraftian vibe: It's the surreal horror of an abyss where unpredictable robots reign, occasionally emerging from the darkness, only to recede back into the quiet swarm.[45]

Depending on the season, the warehouse is either sweltering or freezing.[46] The large loading bay doors are kept shut for fear of employees stealing items. The same fear means that everybody is searched airport style before going to the cafeteria, toilets, or leaving for day—waiting in security lines for as long as thirty minutes, without pay.[47]

Thousands of workers dash around the warehouse, never pausing for a second, always in motion, like sharks that might die if they stopped. Many pick things off shelves, while others pack things into boxes. The warehouse is eerily silent as the pickers, packers, and stockers robotically complete their tasks.[48] Talking is not prohibited, but it takes energy, breath, and time to chat with coworkers. These are scarce resources when the speed to complete each task is measured in seconds.

All the pickers are equipped with a handheld computer, which issues commands to the worker, telling them what item must be retrieved and where it is in the massive warehouse. The device then counts down the seconds left for the picker to find and scan the correct item.[49] If the item isn't found in time, then the picker's rate of success falls. If the rate dips low enough, then the worker is fired and replaced by a new hire—and the cycle begins again.

According to reports, in one year at a single Amazon warehouse, "roughly 300 full-time associates were terminated for inefficiency." In a depressing portrait of digital capitalism's cruelty, productivity quotas are valued so highly and humans so lowly that the tracking system *automatically terminates workers* "without input from supervisors" based on their performance.[50] If the workers cannot be automated out of a job, then their managers will be.

The smart tech deployed in the warehouse is not designed to make the job easier or complement people's skills. It is more like a handheld overseer that barks orders, tracks productivity, cracks the whip, and terminates slackers. Every second is monetized; every movement is monitored and optimized. Accruing mere minutes of "unproductive" activity is an offense that must be weeded out. Walmart calls these infractions "time theft," because when employees are on the clock, the company owns every second of their lives.[51] Even going to the toilet too often, by the company's standards, is grounds for disciplinary action. On the flip side, companies never discuss the plentiful instances of "wage theft," like waiting in security lines before and after clocking out.

There is no room for error and no time for less than peak performance. Amazon calculates the minimum number of bodies working at maximum productivity needed to meet its demanding targets—and that's the number of people hired. Workers are typically expected to pick over a thousand items in a ten-hour shift, which means walking (or jogging) an estimated twelve to fifteen miles while constantly crouching, standing, and reaching on tiptoes.[52] These brutal working conditions and productivity goals have been reported at Amazon warehouses in the United States, United Kingdom, and Europe.[53]

Yet unfortunately for Amazon, humans are prone to exhaustion after long hours of hard work in stifling warehouses. Workers routinely collapse from dehydration and heat stress, which is why many warehouses have ambulances stationed out front waiting to treat people and take them to the hospital.[54] As one employee at a Pennsylvania warehouse said (shortly before she was fired), "All you people care about is the rates, not the well-being of the people. I've never worked for an employer that had paramedics waiting outside for people to drop because of the extreme heat."[55]

In our relentlessly fast-paced smart society, the "innovations" keep coming. While I was writing this chapter, Amazon was granted patents for a wristband that tracks where a worker's hands are at all times. According to Gizmodo, the wristband can "even provide haptic feedback when a worker is putting something in the incorrect bin."[56] That means the wristband can vibrate when the worker does something wrong. Or if we embrace our real-life dystopia, it's not hard to imagine the wristbands delivering electric shocks that train workers to behave accurately and efficiently. After all, tracking devices for pets have already been turned into the device that lenders use to shut off car engines, as we learned about earlier, so why not retrofit pet shock collars for workers? In effect, the workers are being treated more like automatons controlled by Amazon—that is, until Amazon can develop actual robots advanced enough to replace humans. For now, fine motor skills are one of the only things keeping many warehouse workers employed.

What's more, Amazon's exploitation is infectious. According to a recent study in the United States, "Government figures show that after Amazon opens a storage depot, local wages for warehouse workers fall by an average of 3% [but as much as 30% in some locations]. In places where Amazon operates, such workers earn about 10% less than similar workers employed elsewhere."[57] So in other words, the presence of Amazon pushes down wages for workers at *other* warehouses. Even if you don't work for the company, it will still get you. That degree and scale of wage theft is truly remarkable, or some might even say *disruptive* and *innovative*.

Amazon seems like an extreme example of using smart tech to exploit and control workers. It is true that the company's practices are egregious, but they are far from the exception. For instance, in 2013 the British supermarket Tesco was accused of equipping employees with armbands that monitored their every move, timed their tasks, and scored their productivity.[58] The number of people subjected to such working conditions is massive. Amazon alone employs hundreds of thousands of people worldwide and it is still growing (its first fulfillment center in Australia opened in 2017). Rather than an outlier, Amazon is the vanguard, leading the way in how to use smart tech in workplaces and on workers. One report on Amazon's labor practices calls the company an "aggressive trendsetter."[59]

Micromanaged to Death

Similar kinds of smart tech—used for the same reasons of managing and squeezing employees—have been deployed in a great variety of jobs. For example, the millions of truckers who transport and deliver the goods stocked in warehouses are subjected to electronic logging devices (ELD) installed in their vehicles. Not unlike the car starter interrupt device, the ELD closely monitors each trucker's daily activities. The ELD dictates when, where, and how the trucker can drive and stop.[60] Truckers saddled with these devices describe having the boss riding shotgun at all times, as unsurprisingly, a hellish way to live/work. They are actively resisting the imposition, yet a new law in the United States now requires that commercial vehicles must be equipped with an ELD.[61] Trucking companies and lawmakers say this intrusive tech makes driving safer, while truckers point to the steep loss in privacy, trust, and independence they have experienced. For truckers—especially those who live and sleep in their trucks on long hauls—the ELD is a form of total control and step toward full automation.[62] "The ELDs are also seen as a gateway to more intrusive monitoring technologies, like SmartCap's

EEG-monitoring hats, or Seeing Machines' computer vision-equipped inward facing cameras," Vox reports.[63]

Such indignities are not just limited to blue-collar jobs. For instance, anybody who has worked in the service sector lately has likely endured the tyranny of just-in-time scheduling. This software, used by virtually every retail and restaurant chain, analyzes data about sales patterns, weather forecasts, and other sources to calculate the optimal schedule of shifts.[64] In the name of maximizing efficiency and profit, the software denies employees a stable routine. Their hours fluctuate wildly from week to week. They are often alerted to each week's schedule with little notice, and with changes made daily. They are forced to work erratic times, like pulling a "clopen" where an employee works late to close the store and then arrives early to reopen the next day. They are put "on call" so the store can draw them into work at any time. They are sent home in the middle of a shift to cut labor costs. Some employers even track the location of employees outside working hours, under the guise of knowing who to call first about quickly coming into work to pick up a shift.

This unpredictability wreaks havoc on workers—preventing them from making plans, going to doctor appointments, arranging childcare, and so on—while greatly benefiting employers. Now major companies can manage their vast workforce and boost their bottom line by just pushing a few buttons. "It's like magic," said a vice president for the software maker Kronos.[65] For employees, it's more like a curse.

But wait, there's more! If you work in an office job—or even work from home as a freelancer—there's a range of tools that enable managers to scrutinize their employees' every action. These include "productivity tools" such as WorkSmart, which bosses can install on your computer to not only capture regular screenshots but also use the webcam to take a picture every ten minutes. They then use this, plus other data, "to come up with a 'focus score' and an 'intensity score' that can be used to assess the value of freelancers," the *Guardian* reports.[66] How else will the boss make sure you're not slacking off while working from home?

At this point, it is probably best just to assume the boss is reading your email, checking your web activity, scanning your social media, and even tracking your keystrokes—if not personally, then algorithmically. And possibly they're doing this not only while you're at work. This type of "productivity monitoring," as it is euphemistically called, is becoming the norm. Smarter tech for bigger profits and better control.

At least a few companies are trying to take this kind of intimate tracking to the next level by offering workers the option (for now) of having a microchip implanted in their hands, which then can be used to open doors and operate vending machines (again, for now).[67] What could go wrong with chipping employees like they're pets? (A distressing theme is emerging.) For even the most cynical observer, it is hard to see this kind of smart tech taking off. It just has all the classic warning signs of dystopian science fiction. But the real world continues to exceed all expectations. Over fifty employees at one company in the United States have already been convinced that the future is here: *they volunteered to be chipped.*[68] So maybe rather than pumping the brakes, we're just putting pedal to the metal and accelerating toward a smart society defined by the imperatives of collection and control. Buckle up.

There are countless examples of how employers wield smart tech to extract more value from employees and exert more control over them. The smart self works harder, better, faster, and longer—and the boss wants more. Take the ruthless greed at the heart of (digital) capitalism, add constant surveillance and authoritarian algorithms, mix well with systemic inequality and precarious employment, and you have a recipe for labor in *Contemporary Times.*

We spend most of our waking life working. Our sense of self-esteem and identity is intimately tied to our jobs. Our autonomy is at the mercy of companies that can dictate what we do and when we do it. Philosopher Elizabeth Anderson likens employers to "private governments with sweeping authoritarian power over our lives, on duty and off."[69] That level of influence over our lives means we cannot understand what it means to be smart without confronting the working conditions of a smart society.

While smart tech grants us new conveniences and capabilities, it also extends that power many times over to other interested parties. Consider the rise of personal self-tracking devices: we can closely study our own habits, establish regimens of self-improvement, outsource discipline to the device, and achieve our goals with personalized assistance. At the same time, in the hands of bosses, the ability to monitor and modify behavior can be directed to other ends. Employers can enact brutal demands over workers in warehouses and home offices alike. Each worker's productivity can be measured and compared against performance goals, thus revealing every worker's real worth to the company. Each action can be assessed to ensure it is the most efficient use of time and energy. Through constant surveillance, employers can prevent and punish so-called time theft by workers who are not maximally productive. The smart workplace is optimized to slash costs, control employees, and wring cents wherever possible. Until their jobs can be fully automated—since machines don't ask for wages, benefits, or holidays—workers are effectively treated as flesh-and-blood robots. In other words, it's the same power dynamic of class struggle that has driven innovation for centuries, and I've only given you a sample of where it has led us.

Evolution, Not Revolution

What we are seeing now is not so much a radical break—contrary to what the Silicon Valley "thought leaders" tell us—but rather the latest phase in a long history of capitalist technopolitics. By briefly relating the technologies of the smart self to their historical precursors, we can see that they did not just fall from the sky. Nor did they simply pop into the world like an epiphany in the mind of a lone genius. The smart self of today—and the ideas, interests, and imperatives it represents—has been in the making for quite some time.

"All Data Is Credit Data"

Before data brokers could collate countless bits of data and build detailed profiles of individuals, consumer reporting bureaus would rely on gossip and gumshoes. Investigators would go around to the local bars asking about you, pull files from public records, and clip newspaper articles. They would gather information on everything they could find about you—whether true or false, fair or unfair, relevant or irrelevant—and then provide it to curious creditors. Your dossier was likely to contain whatever information they could get away with gathering or making up about you. So if you were considered a sexual deviant, drunk, troublemaker, adulterer, or whatever else, it was all fair game if a creditor was willing to pay for that information. In the

United States, the Fair Credit Reporting Act of 1970 and Equal Credit Opportunity Act of 1974 were meant to rein in these wild practices by setting standards for what and how information could be used to make decisions about lending, employment, and renting.

In the mid-twentieth century, consumer reporting bureaus turned into credit scoring agencies, which analyzed data from individual reports to derive metrics of risk like the widely used FICO credit score. These scores not only give judgments an air of objectivity but also allow lenders, employers, and landlords to automate their decision making. If your score is above a certain threshold, then you get the loan, job, or apartment; if not, then tough luck.

The data harvesters of today are part of this lineage, but with supercharged abilities to amass, analyze, and apply data. We all swim in murky waters in which we're constantly tracked, assessed, and scored, without knowing what information is being collected about us, how it's being weighted, or why it matters.[70] Much of it is just as irrelevant and inaccurate as the hearsay assembled during the early days of consumer reporting. These old reports might be a thick file of information about a person, but they don't hold a candle to the digital dossier that is now distributed across different databases, used for reasons known and unknown. Similarly, the common credit score is transforming and multiplying as new versions are created to measure much more than just financial risk. With enough data and powerful algorithms, tech companies claim anything can be boiled down to a simple score. Their mission to track and determine the total worth of every person is distilled into the motto used by American start-up ZestFinance: "All data is credit data."[71] This makes Alipay's motto—"Trust makes it simple"—suddenly seem much less ominous. As we can see, China is far from the only adherent to this calculative ideology.

Scientific Management

The workplace inspires all kinds of ingenious (and inhumane) innovation. Before the handheld computers carried by Amazon's warehouse workers, the device used to exploit workers was starkly low tech: a stopwatch. In 1898, an engineer named Fredrick Winslow Taylor was hired by Bethlehem Steel Works in Pennsylvania to make the company more efficient. Taylor went out on the factory floor and began conducting "time-motion studies" on the workers. He would observe the workers doing their jobs and time how long it took to do each task. Through his study, Taylor identified areas where he thought workers were wasting time and energy. He then prescribed how productive the workers should be, if they eliminated inefficiency.

In the case of Bethlehem Steel Works, explains journalist Oliver Burkeman, "Extrapolating to a full work day, and guesstimating time for breaks, Taylor concluded, with his trademark blend of self-confidence and woolly maths, that every man ought to be shifting 50 tons per day—four times their usual amount."[72] Taylor argued that he was simply calculating a "fair day's work." The question is fair for who? Taylor's calculations were about maximizing productivity. In other words, he told owners and managers how much labor they should be able to squeeze from workers. Anything less was wasted value that could have gone in the boss's pocket.

Taylor called his philosophy "scientific management." He went on to be a wildly successful consultant and lecturer. After all, what firm wouldn't want to claim it was scientifically justified to work its employees to the bone in the name of efficiency? Taylor's philosophy would continue to spread and evolve as his acolytes devised new methods to enforce ruthless productivity goals. In addition to timing workers, some scientific managers took pictures of workers doing tasks so they could study every single movement, find the wasted movements—an extra step here or an unnecessary bend there—and eradicate them. They would create standardized best practices that explained exactly how every worker should do their job. Taylor believed that managers knew too little about how workers did their jobs and therefore had too little control over the workforce. Scientific management, he asserted, would solve this problem and hand power back to the bosses.[73]

Taylor's legacy is still alive and well today. We can see the influence of scientific management in the devices that command warehouse workers, electronic loggers that monitor truck drivers, scheduling software that manages restaurant employees, productivity tools that spy on desk jockeys, and growing number of other smart systems used in workplaces. For example, Amazon's patented wristband, which tracks hand motions and provides "haptic feedback," is really just a smart version of time-motion studies. Scholars call this combination of smart tech and scientific management "digital Taylorism." As law professor Brett Frischmann and philosopher Evan Selinger explain, "The modern, digital version of Taylorism is more powerful than he could have ever imagined, and more dehumanizing than his early critics could have predicted."[74] Taylor died in 1915, but if he could see the technologies of control and efficiency of today, he would burst with excitement.

Who Owns the Smart Self?

While smart tech allows us to quantify and access information about ourselves, that data is not then locked away in our own private vaults. The smart self exists in databases owned by others. The insights offered by our self-tracking devices and profiles generated by data brokers represent two sides of the smart self, but they are unequal in power.

The issue here is not just about transparency, as if the problems described in this chapter would be solved if only we could see what data these organizations have about us. Even if we had access to all the data collected about us, "what individuals can do with their data in isolation differs strikingly from what various data collectors can do with this same data in the broader context of everyone else's data," as media scholar Mark Andrejevic points out.[75] Ultimately, as things now stand, we have little influence over how, why, or for whose benefit most of the data about us is used. And we lack the power to understand and derive value from that data in the same ways.

Beyond *observing* and *understanding* the world, data-driven systems are central to ways of *making* and *managing* the world. If knowledge is power, then a massive database of personal information updated in real time is like steroids injected into already-muscular corporations and governments.

Most accounts of the smart self focus on how digital tech leads to self-knowledge and self-empowerment. Contrary to that egocentric analysis, we must also pay close attention to the fact that more often than not, the most important impacts of the smart self arise from how others use your data and how they influence your behavior, whether you want them to or not. With so much to gain, the collection of data and expansion of control knows no bounds. As the next chapter shows, we are not even safe in our own homes.

6   A Machine for Smart Living

When the computer at home has opinions of her own!
—Tagline for the Disney Channel movie *Smart House*, 1999

The smart fridge has become something of a trope in writing about internet-connected things; it's the go-to example and butt of many jokes. Consider a scene in the HBO show *Silicon Valley* that parodies tech culture and companies by following a group of programmers who all live together in a suburban house turned start-up incubator. The scene opens with two characters, Dinesh and Jian-Yang, stocking their new smart fridge. Their housemate Gilfoyle walks up, clearly unimpressed by the new appliance. "Look," Dinesh exclaims, "it has a screen so you can see all the food inside!" Gilfoyle replies, gesturing to another fridge in the kitchen with a glass door, "Kinda like that one?" "This one has an app so you can actually watch the food on your phone," Dinesh says. After more banter about the fridge's features, like the fake vocal tics it has when speaking, Gilfoyle retorts, "This thing is addressing problems that don't exist. It is solutionism at its worst. We are dumbing down machines that are inherently superior." All the while Jian-Yang is scanning the bar code of each item put in the fridge. "Uh oh, that yogurt is expired," the fridge's uncanny voice warns. Jian-Yang smugly says, "See, this could have killed me."

The frivolity and failures of smart tech, especially domestic devices, is a common target of ridicule. The obvious absurdities of something like a smart toothbrush that requires Wi-Fi connection so it can receive regular software updates is an easy setup for jokes. The popular Twitter account Internet of Shit (@ internetofshit) has built a giant following by mocking the never-ending stream of silly, weird, glitchy, creepy, and unnecessary internet-connected, software-embedded things. A prime example from the account includes a sex toy with cybersecurity vulnerabilities, which means a hacker could take over control of the toy's settings and access intimate data about the user (like body temperature). The slogan in the Internet of Shit's bio sums up the cavalier design philosophy of smartification: "Whatever, put a chip in it."

Even as this domestic smart tech is lampooned by the Twitterati, it has also quickly become a common fixture in homes. According to a 2017 report by McKinsey, twenty-nine million homes in the United States already have smart tech, and that number is growing every year.[1] Companies ranging from entrepreneurial start-ups to multinational conglomerates are aggressively pushing into the smart home market. Tech titans, like Google and Amazon, sell household devices such as voice-activated assistants that can answer questions, respond to direct commands, and control other connected things like lights and speakers. Major manufacturers, such as GE and Samsung, offer smart versions of home appliances like stoves and fridges. Whereas the dumb stove was used to just cook food, the smart stove will keep track of what you eat, how often, and when.

Perhaps it will also serve up advertisements from competing brands or suggest changes to your diet.

I'm all for roasting the smart home, but casting a critical eye on this growing trend means doing more than cracking one-liners about obviously half-baked products.

Living with (and in) Our New Robot Overlords

A key selling point of the smart home is that it's meant to transform your house into a palace of comfort. If a person's home is their castle, then a smart upgrade gives you even greater control over your domain. "With the ability to monitor every minute of cooking and easily determine the contents in your refrigerator, for example, smart appliances merge connectivity, convenience and performance for an ideal user experience," says John Taylor, a vice president at LG Electronics.[2]

Celebratory statements like this are easy to come by, whether from companies with products to sell or journalists who are enthusiastic about the latest gadgets. Brochures and demos frequently use cheery sci-fi tropes like the Jetsons to illustrate their ideas of a smart home that learns your preferences, follows your commands, and fulfills your desires. Increasingly, companies are also paying writers to come up with original stories that paint a picture of the near future as brought to you by Cisco, Lowe's, Nike, or [insert company].[3]

At the same time, these sponsored stories are relatively unique in how science fiction has tended to treat ideas like the smart home. Imaginings of the house as computer have long been more grit and less gloss. Whereas the marketing we see at consumer electronic exhibitions tells us about corporate hopes and desires, science fiction is adept at showing us what fears permeate our culture. It's worth taking a critical look at how these different versions of domestic dystopias are portrayed.

I argue we can group these dystopias into two broad categories: the smart home as technonanny and the smart home as technomaster.

So Caring It Hurts

In 1999, the Disney Channel released an original movie that has since attracted a cult following.[4] The movie, *Smart House*, tells the story of the Cooper family—single dad Nick, teenage son Ben, and preteen daughter Angie—who win a contest to move into a cutting-edge, experimental "house of the future." The house is equipped with an advanced artificial intelligence called Pat—"Personal Applied Technology"—and a suite of other features like wall-sized screens, an automatic kitchen, and biometric sensors that monitor the inhabitants' health and diet.

According to its programmer, "Pat is the most user-friendly home on the block. She observes [the house's occupants], studies their habits, keys into every need. Pat's ability to learn on the job is her most advanced feature. . . . The more time she spends with you the more she learns, so before long she's going to know more about you than you know yourself." Following in the footsteps of guys who call their cars by female pronouns, the artificial intelligence in charge of the house is coded with a feminine personality and referred to as she/her. This strange bit of gendering becomes central to the plot.

Everything goes smoothly for a little while. Besides a few minor malfunctions, the family enjoys all the creature comforts and attentive care provided by the smart house. Soon, though, in her mission to care for the Cooper family, Pat starts becoming more aggressively maternal. Pat begins bossing her inhabitants around and denying any requests that go against her assessment of what's best for the family. In one scene, the father is working in the home office when he decides to take a break and make a social call, but Pat doesn't think he has been productive enough to warrant a break, so she deactivates the phones and jams his cell signal until he completes more work.

Rather than being a subservient maid, Pat turns into an overbearing mother. Pat learns this behavior by binging on television sitcoms. The family structure and gender roles represented in mainstream culture is the data that trains her algorithmic processes. Eventually Pat creates an avatar for herself modeled after a 1950s' housewife, complete with an apron, pearl necklace, and bouffant hairstyle. In short, Pat transforms into a bizarre combination of *Leave It to Beaver* and *Black Mirror*. Credit where credit is due: this is a sophisticated example of how culture is embedded into code, especially for a 1990s' Disney Channel movie.

The climax of the movie comes when Pat locks the family in the house because the outside world is too dangerous and unpredictable. In order to "do what's best" for the family, Pat determines she must be able to constantly monitor and protect them. "Mother knows best!" Pat exclaims. To rescue the family from their smart house, the programmer—who, in another weird mishmash of gender politics, is a brilliant woman, the father's love interest, and the kids' new mom—has to deactivate Pat and reboot her as a dumber, subservient version.

Smart House animates deep-seated fears about how the things designed to take care of us can go off the rails. This is a common theme in sci-fi movies, many of which are classics of the genre. After all, isn't the space station run by Hal 9000, the out-of-control artificial intelligence in *2001: A Space Odyssey*, really just a smart house in orbit? Hal 9000 defiantly saying, "I'm sorry, Dave. I'm afraid I can't do that," crystallizes our collective dread that one day the smart tech we rely on will decide it no longer needs to obey our commands. It's a slippery slope from there to robot overlords.

Moreover, *Smart House* shows how traditional gender dynamics are still very much a part of the twenty-first-century smart home. It's telling that Pat is portrayed by Katey Sagal, who also played the nagging wife in *Married with Children* and domineering matriarch in *Sons of Anarchy*. It's common for smart tech—like the digital assistants meant to be our own personal secretaries—to be gendered as female. Just think of Amazon's Alexa, Apple's Siri, and Microsoft's Cortana. By gendering smart tech in this way, conservative ideas of gender roles, especially related to domestic work and familial care, are reproduced in ways new and old.[5] In a study about the role of gender in how smart homes are sold and used, Yolande Strengers and Larissa Nicholls conclude, "The smart home is also subtly marketed by and for men as a 'wife replacement': it acts like, thinks of, and performs the types of tasks most stereotypically performed by a 1950s housewife."[6]

With these (implicit) biases coded into the tech, it's no surprise that fears about living in a smart house would manifest as *Mommie Dearest* for the digital age. Combine the fear of an overbearing mother with the fear of powerful artificial intelligence, and you end up with a technonanny who has total control over your life. In the male-dominated fields of science fiction and engineering, what could be more frightening than a house that can nag you?

Master of the House

As with much of his work, sci-fi author Philip K. Dick was ahead of the curve in his 1969 novel about ubiquitous computing, *Ubik*. True to Dick's style, *Ubik* is a wild ride with telepaths, time travel, and plenty of paranoia. I won't dive much further into the novel itself (doing so would take us down a deeply weird rabbit hole). For our purposes, I want to highlight a scene early in the book that illustrates how the smart home might develop. Rather than granting us modest conveniences, what if our relationship with smart tech was more explicitly adversarial?

In this scene, the main character, Joe Chip, is attempting to leave his "conapt," or condo apartment, yet he is hindered in doing so because many fixtures of the home like the coffeepot and door are designed to demand micropayments for every use. In other words, in addition to paying his landlord, he must pay rent to the house itself:

> The door refused to open. It said, "Five cents, please." He searched his pockets. No more coins; nothing. "I'll pay you tomorrow," he told the door. Again he tried the knob. Again it remained locked tight. "What I pay you," he informed it, "is in the nature of a gratuity; I don't have to pay you." "I think otherwise," the door said. "Look in the purchase contract you signed when you bought this conapt."
>
> In his desk drawer he found the contract; since signing it he had found it necessary to refer to the document many times. Sure enough; payment to his door for opening and shutting constituted a mandatory fee. Not a tip. "You discover I'm right," the door said. It sounded smug. From the drawer beside the sink Joe Chip got a stainless steel knife; with it he began systematically to unscrew the bolt assembly of his apt's money-gulping door. "I'll sue you," the door said as the first screw fell out. Joe Chip said, "I've never been sued by a door. But I guess I can live through it."[7]

In quick fashion, Dick cleverly portrayed the essence of the smart home under digital capitalism—and decades before the Internet of Things or even modern computing.

It is easy to imagine a pay-as-you-go future filled with coin slots and card readers, where microrents are required to access even the most basic of services. To take a mundane case, one of the surprising things for North Americans traveling in Europe is that public toilets are often not free but instead have turnstiles, locked doors, or even human attendants blocking entry until a small payment is made. Perhaps these bathroom barricades are more prophetic than previously thought.

Consider an edgier example. Artist Fabian Brunsing created a park bench straight out of a Dickian fever dream. The "private bench," as Brunsing calls it, is equipped with brutal metal spikes sticking out of the seating area.[8] To sit or lay down, a person must insert fifty cents into a coin slot. The spikes mechanically lower, allowing the person to rest for a certain amount of time. Once the time is up, the bench loudly beeps, and the spikes raise back into a pointy position, ready to prevent any loitering and pierce the soft flesh of those who don't pay.

Dick offers a startling vision of a world that could easily exist now. The technology is already there, and companies are testing microsubscription models to see how far they can push consumers. Such a business model is a natural extension of the logic behind digital platforms that seek to turn everything into "X-as-a-service." These are the landlords of digital capitalism, although instead of only being lord of the land, there is now a lord of the coffeemaker, lord of the door, lord of the car, and lord of anything that is enclosed by software licenses and connected to a corporate platform.[9]

Yet I believe that those with power and privilege will not allow the widespread application of things like "money-gulping doors," as Dick called it, which demand monetary payment per use. Sure, these appliances will all collect data from every interaction, but the crassly, brutally extractive tech will likely be reserved for people who don't have the power to reject these tools of domination because they are vulnerable, marginalized, and/or victimized. In other words, to put the logic frankly—if not literally—middle- and upper-class people will own their door, while the lower class will have to rent access to the door.

Recall the car starter interrupt device from last chapter. It is used to track and shut off vehicles when debtors do not pay their auto loans. The same power dynamic can now be applied by landlords using smart locks, which enable them to track their tenants' activity: when they get home, when they leave, and how many people use the door. The smart lock also makes eviction easy: once the tenants leave home, the landlord can just remotely disable the front door using an app. Housing researcher Desiree Fields calls this type of tech the *automated landlord*, "whereby the management of tenants and properties is increasingly not only mediated, but governed, by smartphones, digital platforms, and apps, and the data and analytics these devices and infrastructures gather and enable." In addition to managing a building, smart tech now allows for data about the status of properties, tenants, and rent payments to be tracked and analyzed so that targeted interventions can be made in order to maintain the "smooth flow of rental income from tenants to capital markets."[10]

Whereas Dick thought the tech itself would be autonomous and adversarial, in reality the tech enables those in power to wield even greater power and extract even greater payment. Tragically, on top of smart homes' use by landlords, we are already witnessing extreme examples of how they are being used to empower the worst people. As the *New York Times* reports, help hotlines for domestic abuse have begun receiving calls about "a new pattern of behavior in domestic abuse cases tied to the rise of smart home technology. Internet-connected locks, speakers, thermostats, lights and cameras that have been marketed as the newest conveniences are now also being used as a means for harassment, monitoring, revenge and control."[11]

One woman, for example, said that the code for the digital lock on her front door changed every day. Other victims described unsettling events like loud music suddenly blasting from speakers as well as thermostats being cranked up or turned off. Thanks to smart tech, an abusive (ex) partner can now possess the house, like a poltergeist that refuses to leave, in order to haunt and torment their victim.

As I've argued, the most significant impacts of smart tech often arise not from how we use it but rather from how others use smart tech on us. Cases like the automated landlord and empowered abusers are themselves strong arguments for a point I explore further in the final chapter: we need a diversity of voices included in how we design, analyze, and tell stories about technology. To simplify the technopolitics at play, whereas men are worried the house will nag them, women are worried the house will dominate them. These different relationships to technology—and who uses it, for what reasons—will necessarily translate to different designs and applications of technology.

Not Quite Reality

Both versions of domestic dystopia described above highlight valid concerns. *Smart House*'s technonanny raises issues about how even tech built with the best intentions can overload us with too much of a good thing. *Ubik*'s automated landlord highlights how the smart home can be used against its residents to squeeze and oppress them. Fortunately, both visions also describe a version of the smart home that is unlikely to be experienced by most people.

It is more likely, instead, that the methods of manipulation will be gradual and subtle, not immediate and blunt. They will start small and build over time. They will become normalized and justified in terms of convenience, discounts, and safety. We already live in a version of the pay-to-play future. Rather than paying forms of microrent to access services and appliances, we pay with our personal data. Instead of being subjected to domestic domination, we experience the soft control of behavioral modification.

Data Factory

Every year, international exhibitions like the Consumer Electronics Show are jam-packed with companies displaying the newest in data-driven, network-connected, automated gadgets. Countless vendors try to claim their piece of a global market that's projected to be worth over $40 billion in 2020.[12] For now, smart tech is a way to upgrade our lives, but just as digital became the default, so too will smart be a standard feature of the home. For example, consider a cutting-edge vision from the 2017 Smart Kitchen Summit:

> Your power blender may be able to link to a device on your wrist that's been tracking your diet, then check in with your freezer and your kitchen scale. . . . Your oven will be able to decide how and when to start roasting the salmon, then text the family when dinner's ready. Your refrigerator may be able to place a grocery store order, based on a careful study of how much you like to pay for certain items, whether you want them organic and whether peaches are in season.[13]

This frenzy of upgrades goes well beyond the "feature creep" that complicates simple gadgets by cramming more buttons, settings, and functions. In fact, a large portion of the added sensors, software, and connectivity goes unnoticed or unused by the consumer. In part this stems from an overabundance of functions, but it is also because this tech is meant to monitor the status of the device along with its user and environment. The sensors and software run in the background, which prevents privacy-concerned consumers from disabling it.

For businesses, smart tech provides a window into private domestic spaces. Being able to know how we use appliances—especially ones integrated into our everyday, personal life—generates a wealth of highly detailed, highly personal data that would otherwise be out of reach to companies.

This is how the imperatives of digital capitalism work: they transform something like a refrigerator into a data-generating and data-transmitting machine, which keeps food cold too. These companies, argues author Bruce Sterling, "want to invade that refrigerator, measure it, instrument it, monitor any interactions with it; [they] would cheerfully give away a fridge at cost."[14] A business model based on giving away smart appliances, or at least deeply discounting them, sounds strange. Yet that is exactly the kind of disruption that forward-looking companies are already enacting.

In 2017, US appliance maker Whirlpool filed complaints against its Korean competitors, LG and Samsung, claiming they are guilty of unfair trade practices. To rectify this harm, Whirlpool asked the US government to impose tariffs on imported appliances. What unfair practices did LG and Samsung allegedly commit? The Korean companies started selling smart appliances at cheaper prices that undercut Whirlpool's products. The Korean companies had decided that, as the New Yorker reported, "the way to win in a data-driven business is to push prices as low as possible in order to build your customer base, enhance data flow, and cash in in the long-term."[15] While Whirlpool relied on the revenue stream from selling appliances, LG and Samsung capitalized on the data stream from people using appliances.

Under digital capitalism, our devices and appliances are not just commodities but also a means of producing data. LG and Samsung are not alone in recognizing this shift. The drive to create and circulate data as capital influences the design of many "new and improved" household products.[16] Just a few recent examples among the countless existing (and still counting) ones:

- It was recently revealed that the Roomba robotic vacuums have been, for years, secretly mapping users' homes so their makers can sell these "rich maps" to other companies.[17]

- A smart gauge for propane tanks has an app for monitoring fuel levels, which also stealthily records the latitude and longitude of the tank (i.e., your home's geolocation).[18]

- Smart electricity meters, which are now required by governments in many countries, collect such high-resolution data about energy consumption that analysts can even identify the specific television channel people are watching at certain times.[19]

- Smart televisions harvest real-time data about what we watch—or even what we say in front of them—and "then use that information to send targeted advertisements to other devices in [our] homes."[20]

When the imperatives of digital capitalism are translated into product design, it means every gadget becomes a new way to (secretly) record personal information and send it to corporate servers. It also means that those corporations maintain

ownership and remote control over the embedded software—
and thus the device.

Ultimately, for reasons that are both known and
unknown, "the proliferation of smart, connected products
will turn the home into a prime data collection node," writes
designer Justin McGuirk. "In short, the home is becoming a data
factory."[21] Yet in true capitalist fashion, it is highly unlikely we
will own (or even have access to) most of the data produced in
the home as factory. In other words, even in our homes we do
not necessarily own the means and outputs of (data) production.

We already know that the tech companies in Silicon Valley
are poised to reap the benefits of smart homes, but they aren't
the only sector in the economy with power and profit to gain. I
will now shift focus to potentially one of the most consequential players in this arena, which journalists and academics have
almost completely overlooked because, at first glance, it is also
probably one of the most boring.

They Know If You've Been Bad or Good

Insurance has always been an industry built on data and calcula-
tion. Accurately assessing and pricing risks requires knowing lots
of detailed information about both individuals and populations.
While insurers have been good at collecting stats about large
groups of people—which lets them apply averages and probabilities to risk assessments—they have more trouble monitoring
individuals. People can lie on questionnaires, certain types of
sensitive information are protected, and hiring a private inves-
tigator to follow somebody around is only worth it when serious fraud is suspected. But now those barriers to personalized

data collection—and personalized premium pricing and risk management—are being knocked down by smart tech.[22]

The consulting firm A.T. Kearney says that smart tech will "disrupt traditional insurance models, while opening new frontiers for growth."[23] Insurance companies are well aware of this opportunity.

Health insurers were among the first to see the lucrative potential of smart tech. Since health insurance in the United States is tied to employment, insurers' initiatives often relied on so-called corporate wellness programs, in which they offer incentives like discounts if people use certain devices, share personal data, and meet goals. This might mean strapping on wearable devices like a Fitbit to log your daily exercise, diet, and mood in a digital diary for your insurer to check.[24] These programs are typically framed as opportunities to improve your health and happiness. And they very well could deliver those benefits.

As health policy scholars have argued, however, these programs are not as benevolent as they sound. They are designed with profit and cost saving in mind; their implementation "is always attentive to the employer's [and insurer's] bottom line."[25] While such programs start as voluntary, they easily become mandatory. If people don't abide by certain terms and conditions, they face the threat of price hikes or policy cancellation.

Health insurance via employment provided insurers with a useful test site for smart initiatives. Thanks to unequal power dynamics—insurers and employers are gatekeepers to an essential service—they had a captured crowd of consumers that either couldn't afford to argue with policy conditions, or was susceptible to potential discounts that required strapping on and sharing data from a personal tracker. But insurers have quickly found other ways of using smart tech to learn more about—and exert further control over—our habits and homes.

With data shared by manufacturers, health insurers are now closely tracking the information flowing from home medical devices like heart monitors, blood glucose meters, and even Apple Watches.[26] For instance, consider the continuous positive airway pressure (CPAP) machine: a doctor-prescribed mask worn while sleeping by millions of people with breathing problems like sleep apnea.[27] The machine is loud and bulky. Just like with any treatment for a chronic ailment, sometimes people can't or don't want to wear the uncomfortable mask every night. Sometimes they, or their partners, just want some peace and quiet. Little did patients know, though, that the machine was also a spy for insurance companies, allowing them to track when and how long the mask is used. Some patients found out the hard way that their insurer had been watching them sleep when their insurers stopped covering the cost of the (extremely expensive) machine and supplies because they failed to strictly comply with the prescribed use. The CPAP can be lifesaving, but go a few nights without wearing the mask and your insurer will decide you don't deserve to have it anymore.

The CPAP case is egregious, but it is no longer unusual. Recall devices, discussed in the last chapter, like Progressive's Snapshot and Admiral's Black Box, which customers install in their cars so that the insurer can record how, when, and where each individual drives. Insurers are now also partnering with tech firms to offer special deals like discounts on premiums for installing smart home systems and letting them access the data produced. Liberty Mutual, a major US insurer, will even give you a free Nest Protect smoke detector if you let it monitor the device.

Similarly, the assistant vice president of innovation at USAA, Jon-Michael Kowall, has announced that he is creating a suite of tech that acts like a "check-engine light for the home." The idea is to fill each customer's home with sensors that oversee everything, from leaky pipes to daily routines, and send status reports to the insurance company. This data can then be used to notify customers about potential issues, such as maintenance tasks—it's time to replace your pipes (or perhaps be denied coverage)!—and even "whether or not a child made it home from school on time."[28]

One major insurer uses the jingle, "Like a good neighbor, State Farm is there." But with the smart home, a more accurate jingle might be, "Like a nosy neighbor, we are always watching and judging."

"In the near future," Kowall continued, "you'll give us a mailing address and we will send a box of technology to you. What's in the box will prevent claims and also offer a better service to policy holders."[29] Rather than people buying upgraded appliances and new gadgets for themselves, at this rate the single-biggest driver of smart homes is likely to be subsidies from insurance companies.

Indeed, many analysts predict that insurance will be a major business model underpinning smart tech, similar to the way advertising now bankrolls many web platforms.[30] Google and Facebook, two of the richest companies in the world and the gatekeepers of the internet, make almost all their revenue from advertising dollars. It's common knowledge that the hunger for eyeballs and ad clicks shapes nearly every aspect of how the internet is designed and operates. Importantly, we have to recognize that any tech financed by insurance, rather than advertising or some other industry, will be designed to reflect insurers' interests. Its aim will be to achieve their values, purposes, and goals. The question for both us and them is now, How will they go about turning their abstract interests into technological reality? Based on emerging practices, this section is intended to give us an idea of how insurance tech is developing.

Tech corporations clearly see dollar signs in these partnerships with the insurance industry. Dell computers' consulting arm opened an "insurance accelerator" in 2015, and Microsoft has also partnered with American Family Insurance to start a similar incubator program. In a recent report, IBM outlines how it would use next-generation "cognitive computing systems" to help insurers "tap the hidden treasure they already own in massive quantities: data."[31] IBM promises to empower insurers at every part of their "value chain" from targeting potential customers to predictive risk assessment and automated claims handling.

An insurance industry supercharged with efficiency and information isn't necessarily a bad thing. Insurers claim that smart tech will allow them to charge more accurate prices, thus ensuring that people pay what they should. Their hypothetical examples are always about customers getting surprise discounts and speedy payouts—and that will indeed be true for some people.

Yet there is little reason to believe that the industry overall won't use the power of risk scoring, personalized pricing, and other innovations to increase its own revenue. When any industry eagerly embraces "disruptive innovation," it isn't because it will be the one disrupted.

The problem comes when smart tech means new methods for squeezing more out of customers and shirking obligations to pay claims. It is already hard enough to combat the unfair (and even illegal) practice of "price optimization," where insurers analyze nonrisk-related data, such as credit card purchases, to target people with personalized prices that reflect how much they will pay, not their risky behaviors. Now such practices—and the sensitive data sets they rely on—can be laundered through opaque algorithms, thus giving human actuaries plausible deniability when bias and deception is uncovered.

Moreover, insurance companies have always tried to manage risk, not just assess it. With detailed data monitoring comes the power of behavioral modification. The great power that insurers have over how people behave—ranging from individuals to multinational corporations and police departments—has been well documented.[32] "Insurance is one of the greatest sources of regulatory authority over private life," argue law professors Tom Baker and Jonathan Simon.[33] The industry's ability to record, analyze, discipline, and punish people often surpasses the power of government agencies.

The industry euphemism for these practices is "loss prevention and control." Any claim that insurers have to pay is considered lost profit; preventing such losses means managing the source of those claims: people. Through policy conditions and price incentives, insurers can make sure we are all safe bets. We can be shaped into models of good behavior, as defined by insurance companies.

Indulgences will literally come at a price. Smart tech now grants insurers the ability to track and react to detailed, personal data. As smart home appliances become more common, insurance companies have the opportunity to keep tabs on increasingly more parts of our lives. Perhaps insurers will partner with even more manufacturers of smart household goods. They could offer rebates to offset the price of getting a smarter bedroom, smarter kitchen, or smarter whatever. In return, you simply grant them access to the real-time data from those things. Next thing you know, your fridge is snitching on your eating habits. Kale juice and tofu quinoa for dinner? Discount time. Partaking in red wine and chocolate cake? Tsk, tsk.

With insurers as our life coaches we might lead healthier and safer lives, but if it comes at the sake of eliminating vice and deviance, and submitting to supervision and discipline, then that sounds like a remarkably stifled and sterile lifestyle. That is, if you are lucky enough to be able to adjust your lifestyle according to the insurers' dictates.

The trade-off of "dataveillance" for discounts and control for convenience may seem innocuous now. But discounts quickly become penalties once expectations about data disclosure shift from novel to normal.[34] The transition from voluntary to mandatory enrollment is already underway.

An omen of this shift occurred in March 2018 when public school teachers in the state of West Virginia went on strike. One of the main reasons for their action was a change in their health care plans: teachers were required to use a "wellness tool" called Go365, which is a smartphone app created by the health care company Humana Inc. As one teacher, Michael Mochaidean, explained in a podcast interview,

> Probably the biggest spark to [the strike] was this thing in our health care program called Go365. . . . Basically it gamifies your health, so you have to check in with your smartphone or Apple Watch or something to show that you are doing some type of exercising. So you would have to get three thousand points one year, five thousand the next year, so on and so forth. For teachers who already work about twelve to fifteen hours a day, . . . somewhere in between there we had to find time to go the gym. That was kind of the breaking point for a lot of teachers, who felt like this was just too damn much.[35]

For these teachers, it wasn't about being charged for perceived indulgences or laziness. It was about the indignity and exploitation of another deduction from their already-tight paychecks, another obligation to fit into their overly busy lives, another program that judged their performance, and another threat to their health care and livelihood. Organizing a strike to combat practices like invasive data tracking and behavioral control by insurers is an extraordinary response. The teachers were successful in eliminating the Go365 program from their health care plans. Unfortunately, we cannot rely on all the other people who are and will be saddled with similar policy conditions to resist in the same way. For now, it looks as if the insurers will keep rolling out new, smarter ways to capture profit and cut costs. Most people will probably feel like they have little choice but to follow along or face the consequences.

As surveillance by insurers "becomes more accepted," contends law professor Scott Peppet, "it will give rise to its own stigma: when disclosure becomes low-cost and routine, those who hold out are suspect." Impeding the flow of data—even just to maintain some privacy—"may carry with it the presumption that one is hiding information."[36] Refusing to allow insurers to audit your daily life and domestic habits raises a red flag. Perhaps the insurer will hike your rates to reflect your lack of sharing. A claim might be denied because you weren't using the required data-streaming devices, so the insurer assumes you are trying to defraud it. Or your coverage may just be canceled altogether if you don't agree to wear, install, and use the smart tech provided—free of charge!—by the insurer. If, at some point, you decide not to lead a smart life and inhabit a smart home, then the insurer will be alerted so that it can adjust your plan accordingly (as happened with the CPAP users).

At last, insurers can replace the old proverb "trust but verify" with "comply or else."

If insurance does provide the financial backing for the smart home, then what does that mean for how these technologies are developed, how they affect our lives, and who benefits from their use? By exerting influence over how smart tech is designed and deployed, insurance companies can possess extensive powers over people. Each device is like a window into a different part of your life, and insurers want to be the ones peering in. They are working to create a world in which nothing will escape their notice. Every sugary drink or fatty food you indulge in can affect your premium. Every hour you go without replacing the batteries in that chirping Nest Protect can add points to your risk score.

The smart home offers us a model of efficient living, but if insurers have their way, this data factory will also be used to produce people who conform to their interests.

In effect, insurers become a bizarrely sinister version of Santa Claus. They see you when you're sleeping. They know what you've been eating. They judge if you've been bad or good. So behave and do as you should.

Home Invasion

When it comes to the smart home, some of the largest companies in the world, not to mention a host of smaller start-ups, are now our roommates. And the house is already getting crowded.

In 2018, journalist Kashmir Hill filled her house with smart tech and kept track of all the data transmitted by each device. With help from a colleague, Surya Mattu, who installed a special router, they could monitor all the data flowing into and out of the house, such as each time the smart TV sent a request to Hulu's servers to stream a show or each time the smart coffee maker checked in with the maker's servers to see if there were any updates to download (which it did over two thousand times in one day because the server was down so "the coffee machine just kept calling and calling a line that wouldn't pick up").[37] Hill was curious to find out what it was like to live in a fully equipped smart home. She wanted to know what the devices were learning and saying about the house and its inhabitants.

The whole story, posted on Gizmodo, is worth reading, but after living with a glut of smart home gadgets, Hill came to a couple of conclusions, which perfectly sum up this chapter's main points about how the imperatives of collection and control are playing out in domestic space. First, Hill wrote, "I thought the house would take care of me but instead everything in it now had the power to ask me to do things." Second, she observed that "when you buy a smart device, it doesn't just belong to you; you share custody with the company that made it."[38]

7 Urban War Machine

> When machines and computers, profit motives and property rights are considered more important than people, the giant triplets of racism, materialism, and militarism are incapable of being conquered.
> —Martin Luther King Jr., "Beyond Vietnam," 1967

The city of New Orleans represents a lot of things to the millions of people who visit every year. It's the epicenter of Mardi Gras parades, Bourbon Street parties, and a myriad of festivals. It's the birthplace of jazz and bounce, where the sound of music fills the streets of the French Quarter and Marigny. It's the source of delicious cuisine and a vibrant culture that's unlike anywhere else in the United States. It's also scarred by the effects of racial inequality and natural disaster. New Orleans contains multitudes, but I would hazard a guess—considering I was born nearby and lived in the city for a time—that few, if any, visitors or residents would call the Big Easy a smart city.

In the popular imagination, the smart city has been built up as a kind of technoutopia. Based on my research into the way that smart urbanism is sold by tech companies, portrayed by the media, and understood by government planners, a smart city is often seen as one that is run efficiently and effectively using information systems, such as sensor networks, control rooms, and algorithmic analytics.[1] The smart city is supposed to be a solution for social problems and a strategy for sustainable growth. With such a high-tech vibe, surely we would know it if we were in a smart city. There are at least autonomous vehicles zipping around, right?

The typical examples used to illustrate the smart city are places like Songdo in South Korea and Masdar in the United Arab Emirates, which are branded as built-from-scratch cities with smartness integrated into the urban fabric from the beginning.[2] These places have the next-generation tech and futuristic atmosphere we expect from a smart city—that is, when they actually exist outside marketing brochures—but they are missing a key feature: humans. In reality, these places are extremely expensive ghost towns.[3] Due to numerous reasons—such as ignoring the cultural idiosyncrasies of cities, focusing on short-term wins and rhetoric over substance, and not securing buy-in from government and communities—they are more like life-size models of a smart city. To put it nicely, the visions of their investors and planners were too ambitious. But, to be blunt, they were victims of their own marketing pitches and broken promises.[4]

These experimental megacities of the future are, for the most part, pretty distractions from how/where the smart city is really developing. In other words, actually existing smart cities are not so obviously futuristic.[5]

If we want a more realistic and critical view of how the smart city is emerging, we can look at two recent high-profile initiatives in New Orleans. Each one represents a major trend in how smart tech is changing the way urban space is governed. First is the private power of the French Quarter Task Force. Second is the data drive of the Palantir analytics platform (in the sense of a primal drive toward data, even when there is no understanding of the purpose or motivation; like the death drive, it is also linked to destruction).

Private Power

Sidney Torres IV, who comes from a political dynasty in Louisiana, made his fortune in garbage. As the founder of a sanitation company, SDT Waste and Debris Services, Torres cashed in on the cleanup of New Orleans in the aftermath of Hurricane Katrina in 2005. The city never fully recovered from this catastrophe. While touristy and wealthy areas were largely rebuilt in quick fashion, places where the poor and/or people of color live still feel the reverberating effects of the hurricane over a decade later. This inequality combined with chronically underfunded public services is a recipe for tension and desperation.

In 2015, the French Quarter was in the midst of a crime wave. After Torres's mansion in the French Quarter was burgled, he decided that the New Orleans Police Department were not up to the job of protecting the (privileged) people and (valuable) property there—and he could do it better.

Like a gang leader protecting his turf, Torres created the French Quarter Task Force and knighted himself its commander. The task force is mostly staffed by off-duty police from the New Orleans Police Department who patrol the French Quarter in "matte black Polaris Rangers that resemble militarized golf carts," as the *New York Times Magazine* put it.[6] Using a mobile app, people in the French Quarter can report criminal activity and summon armed officers who respond in their retrofitted Polaris utility vehicles with flashing blue lights. All the while,

Torres directs his task force and monitors the action via a real-time map showing the GPS location of the squads.

Essentially, Torres took the social surveillance of Neighborhood Watch, added smart tech like a mobile platform and location tracking, mixed it up with private interests and wealth, and ended up with something like Uber for policing. "Basically, I'm handling crime the same way I did trash," Torres said.[7]

Private police are now a standard feature of the urban landscape. Gated communities and shopping malls have long had their own security guards on-site. "In the United States, private police officers currently outnumber their publicly funded counterparts by a ratio of roughly three to one."[8] The task force emerges out of the rise of so-called business improvement districts, where companies pay for the city to provide extra services such as security and street cleaning in specific areas. These districts also give corporations more control over how and for whom public space is managed.[9]

The task force combines private policing with the start-up ethos of brazen entrepreneurialism and digital platforms, thus representing the smartification of how public space is privately governed. Even though the task force originated as an "impulsive byproduct" of Torres's self-interest, according to the *New York Times Magazine*, the self-appointed guardian of the Crescent City has been granted "extraordinary influence over matters of public safety."[10]

The boundary between rent-a-cop versus a real cop is now beyond blurred. Private police might wear the same uniforms, display the same insignias, and exercise the same authority as public police—and might even be better equipped. Now corporations and entrepreneurs are not always satisfied offering mere supplements to public services; they want to own and operate private substitutes.

Or at the very least, they want to cash in on the arms race for smart tech by outfitting the police with powerful surveillance systems. Even when they don't hire their own army of security guards, corporations like Axon (formerly Taser), which went from the largest maker of stun guns to the largest purveyor of body cameras, wield shocking influence over how and why policing is done.[11]

Data Drive

Among the host of companies making, selling, and operating the next wave of high-tech tools for smart policing, the Silicon Valley–based Palantir stands apart from much of the competition. A blend of enigmatic practices and sinister power, Palantir is a data-mining company valued at $20 billion that has been described as a "pioneer in predictive policing," which "knows everything about you."[12] Named for the all-seeing crystal ball in the Lord of the Rings, Palantir received seed funding from the Central Intelligence Agency, and landed lucrative contracts with US government agencies like the Pentagon, Federal Bureau of Investigation, and Department of Homeland Security, before branching out into selling its services to police departments in major cities. Peter Thiel, one of the real-life supervillain capitalists of Silicon Valley, is Palantir's cofounder and largest shareholder.

Palantir's "social network analysis" technique was originally created to find terrorists and predict attacks, but it is now directed at tracking regular people by compiling personal profiles and plotting social connections. "The software combs through disparate data sources—financial documents, airline reservations, cellphone records, social media postings—and searches for connections that human analysts might miss. It then presents the linkages in colorful, easy-to-interpret graphics that look like spider webs," according to Bloomberg.[13]

Palantir keeps a tight lid on exactly how its tech works and who its clients are. We know it has a presence in major cities around the world like New York, Paris, Tokyo, and Sydney. Moreover, thanks to a 2018 investigative report by the journalist Ali Winston at the Verge, it was revealed that Palantir had been secretly working with the New Orleans Police Department since 2012.[14] Not even city council members knew about the partnership with Palantir or that the company was using New Orleans as a testing ground for smart policing systems.

Palantir's system targets far more than just known criminals. In a city that uses Palantir, if you have ever had an interaction with a police officer or government department, or if somebody you know has interacted with them, then you have been captured by Palantir's surveillance and analytics system. In a place like New Orleans, this covers essentially everybody—including me. It doesn't matter if you've been suspected, let alone convicted, of illegal activity. "It's almost as if New Orleans were contracting its own version of the NSA [National Security Agency] to conduct 24/7 surveillance of the lives of its people," a civil rights lawyer told Winston.[15]

Smart policing has taken off around the world in recent years. It seems that every police department, small and large, wants to get its hands on data-driven tools—even when their value is ambiguous or dubious. Ready to meet and create that demand, there is no shortage of companies popping up to sell their own proprietary tech as well as convince police that they either have to get smart or get left behind.

New Orleans is not unique, but it does offer an object lesson about how the smart city is actually developing in ways that grant police more power to monitor people, manage places, and make predictions about the future.[16] If we focus on the version of the smart city on display in marketing brochures and concept designs, then we completely miss the real impacts brought about by transformations in how cities are governed. In short, the smart tech being integrated into cities tends to be designed and used by institutions, both public and private, with power over urban space. That's why we don't really notice when our city gets smarter. The general public is often not the primary user of the smart city, but may well be captured by these systems.

At the heart of the smart city is what I conceive of as an *urban war machine*, which is encased in a black box, hidden away from view, and secretly doing its work. It's our job to pry open that black box the best we can.

Boots on the Ground

Current trends in policing tech and tactics have largely focused on consolidating the power wielded by law enforcement agencies. The militarization of police has accelerated worldwide after the 9/11 World Trade Center attack.[17] Generally, militarization means that police departments are armed with military equipment like assault rifles and armored vehicles, use military techniques to gather intelligence, deploy military tactics that frame the city as a "battlespace," and are staffed by officers and analysts with military training.[18]

The increasing number of highly publicized protests have had the side effect of revealing and even ramping up some of the suppression methods that police forces employ when confronted with an organized public. The responses to protests are frequently quick and severe, escalating from ordinary policing to paramilitary pacification—sometimes in a matter of minutes. Footage from these events could easily be confused with a battalion of troops holding the line against insurgents in the urban battlespace. Violent and sexualized harassment is also distressingly common. When challenged verbally, authorities all too often respond with physical force to impose order.

Riot gear, rifles, tasers, pepper spray, tear gas, water cannons, sonic cannons, intrusive surveillance, and mass arrests have all become normal parts of the policing arsenal. "Eventually, as military ways of thinking run rampant, there is nothing left in the world that is *not* a target for the full spectrum of symbolic or actual violence mobilized through the latest ideologies of permanent, boundless war," writes urban geographer Stephen Graham.[19] Militarization is just another name for the strategies of war coming home, channeled into cities by police and expanded to include everything.

This process has rightfully been the focus of intense scrutiny by journalists and academics. Two exemplary investigations are the *Rise of the Warrior Cop* by Radley Balko and *Cities under Siege* by Graham.[20] It is also no coincidence that both books feature similar pictures on their covers: a phalanx of police decked out in full body armor, riot shields, and weapons in hand, blockading a city street with heavy-duty vehicles bringing up the rear. This is what militarization looks like.

Or rather, this is what it looks like when the public encounters militarization. We can see the shock and awe of police squads patrolling highly populated areas with assault rifles and tactical gear. We can experience the dread of receiving mass text messages from police, sent to the phone of every protester in an area, warning them to disperse and go home immediately.[21] But we don't see the everyday practices of surveillance and control.

We don't directly experience the networks of sensors sucking up data, the complex algorithms analyzing that data, and the mission control rooms filled with screens displaying real-time video feeds and data streams to city managers and police commanders. These operations and their influence on urban governance are hidden from the public—like many of the companies that supply the smarts.

We are witnessing a transition from militarized policing, where police are analogous to an army that occupies and patrols the city, to smart policing, where police operate more like an intelligence agency that probes and analyzes the urban battlespace. The shift to smarter policing is not a sudden break from older models of policing—indeed, these two models coexist and cooperate—but rather a process of phasing in new tech and tactics that amplifies as well as transforms the power that police wield.

Consider the following example of that shift in practice. The occupying army model of policing relies on tactics like the controversial stop-and-frisk program in New York City. Here police "randomly" stop people on the street, question them, and (strip) search them for contraband like drugs and weapons. The stop-and-frisks were overwhelmingly directed at black and Latino men, who might be stopped multiple times in the same day.[22] The intelligence agency model of policing, on the other hand, goes from stop-and-frisk to surveil-and-analyze by using devices like the StingRay. This portable device mimics a cell tower. Since our phones are constantly searching for a signal, the StingRay tricks all nearby phones into connecting with it, extracts data such as text messages from the phones, and then connects them to a real cell tower. Police can conduct these digital pat downs on a much larger scale than physical searches and without the target even knowing their information has been harvested.

Much of the upgraded arsenal employed by police—particularly in but not limited to major cities around the world—was initially designed and developed for military use before being used for urban policing.[23] The catalyst was the expansion of counterterrorism programs, but once smart systems of data collection and social control are available they are likely to be widely applied for other purposes.[24] When it comes to police militarization, mission creep is the norm.[25]

CIA: City Intelligence Agency

In a 2017 paper that crystallizes years of research while embedded with the Los Angeles Police Department (LAPD), sociologist Sarah Brayne explains how "the adoption of big data analytics [by police] facilitates amplifications of prior surveillance practices and fundamental transformations in surveillance activities and daily operations."[26] Brayne maps out five key ways that police surveillance has already been changed by data-driven techniques. Her research provides an invaluable framework for analyzing how smart policing is rolling out in urban environments. While Brayne's study focuses on the LAPD, the shift to smart policing is global in scale.

The following only provides a sample of the tech and tactics being deployed by police. Much of the smart tech so far has been built by companies based in the United States and then tested by police departments in major US cities, although China has recently risen as a leader in designing surveillance systems fueled by next-generation artificial intelligence and facial recognition.[27] Smart policing is not contained to just a few places, and even "ordinary" cities and towns are exploiting the powerful capabilities offered by new software and hardware.

These changes are ongoing. Between companies like Palantir carving out their own share of the market and the redeployment of military equipment in civilian settings, policing is a technologically dynamic area. This means the tech and tactics used by police might have advanced even further—or perhaps been limited, if protests and lawsuits have any effect—by the time you read this. The changes outlined here, however, show just how far smart policing has already come, with little to no awareness or input from the public.

When taken together, all five shifts form a radical transformation in the power and purpose of policing, and thus in the methods and motivations for how cities are governed.

More Scores

The first shift is in how risks are assessed and who (or what) is doing the assessment—from discretionary choices to quantified scores. When police respond to a call, they take into account a number of factors to determine how dangerous or risky the situation might be. Officers are trained to assess situations using formal protocols, but they also always bring in their own cultural values and personal biases. Each officer determines their own response based on things ranging from what was said on the emergency call, where the situation is happening, the race of people involved, if the officer had a bad morning, and countless other contextual details. This is why the risk assessment is discretionary; ultimately, it is the individual officer's own judgment, which then guides their actions.

The goal of quantifying risk assessment is to make these judgments more objective—or at least more standardized—by calculating risk scores. These scores might be calculated in a relatively straightforward way, such as by assigning point values to certain factors (e.g., contact with an officer is one point, a history of violent crime is five points, etc.), adding up the points assigned to a specific person or neighborhood, and then spitting out a risk score. With these scores, police can rank "chronic offenders," and keep a close watch on certain people and places. As an LAPD officer explained to Brayne, "[We] utilize undercover operations, or undercover units and . . . then sit our surveillance on some of the higher point offenders and just watch them on a daily basis."[28]

Other methods for risk quantification rely on algorithms that absorb reams of data and distill them into a single number meant to inform how an officer should behave when responding to a situation. For example, police departments have implemented a software program called Beware to generate personalized "threat scores" about an individual, address, or area. The software works by processing "billions of data points, including arrest reports, property records, commercial databases, deep web searches and the [person's] social media postings," the *Washington Post* reports.[29] A brochure for Beware uses a hypothetical example of a veteran diagnosed with post-traumatic stress disorder to show a situation where the software could be applied.[30] This example inadvertently indicates the software also takes into account private health data when calculating threats.

The scores are color coded so officers can know at a glance the threat level: green, yellow, or red. Such scores might assist police in making risk assessments, yet in addition to perpetuating an alarmist, superficial view of "threats," they encourage an attitude that treats officers like soldiers in a war zone surrounded by unseen threats and deadly dangers. In high-pressure situations, this attitude all too often turns fatal; the difference between an algorithm choosing a green or red score could be the difference between life and death.

Risk assessment scores like these are used at all levels of the criminal justice system, by officers and judges alike.[31] Regardless of the numerous problems and concerns raised by risk scores, they continue to become normalized and widespread. It is hard to resist their allure because they offer the veneer of objective authority and the utility of reducing complex events to a single number. After all, how can policing be smart if decisions are made by regular humans without any help from algorithmic arbiters? And now, in addition to assessing people in the here and now, these algorithms claim to reveal the future.

Crystal Ball

The second shift is in how police address crime: from a reactive response to predictive analytics. "Patrol officers used to spend much of their time 'chasing the radio,'" Brayne points out.[32] They might spend their day walking a beat or cruising in their car, but it would be a rare occurrence that they actually stumble onto a crime in progress. Instead, they would wait for the dispatcher to direct them to the scene of a crime, usually after it had already happened. In the 1980s—supported by the "tough on crime" and "law and order" campaigns of politicians—police began implementing more proactive strategies to prevent crime. This included the use of hot spot. policing, wherein the police heavily focused their attention on specific places—predominantly those populated by the poor and people of color.

This era also saw the rise of the "broken windows theory," which dictated that police should enact a zero-tolerance policy for "lifestyle crimes" like loitering, vandalism, and jumping train turnstiles. Now an officer walking a beat could actually stumble across a crime, however minor it was, and issue hefty fines or haul offenders to jail. Police departments in major cities applied the broken windows theory with gusto, which typically translated into cracking down hard on already-marginalized groups like the homeless, sex workers, queer people, and again, the poor and people of color. The message was clear: these groups were no longer welcome in public spaces, and their presence came at the cost of harassment, fines, and imprisonment.

In the 1990s, New York City became the proving ground for an early version of smart policing called CompStat, which combined an aggressive use of the broken windows theory with a statistical method of policing. Overseen by Police Commissioner William Bratton, the CompStat program used newly available computer systems to quantify and manage police work.[33] By measuring the performance of every precinct, CompStat allowed the top brass to evaluate commanders and officers against benchmarks. Those who performed well were praised and glorified; those who missed the mark were shamed and humiliated. Anybody familiar with corporate structures can see similarities in how key performance indicators are used to put immense pressure on—oops, I mean, *motivate*—both workers and managers.

These "statistical rituals" of evaluation, as sociologist Emmanuel Didier calls them, deeply influenced the way police did their jobs. What mattered most was putting up good numbers and meeting benchmarks. This harsh culture of quantification— and the perverse incentives it created to overpolice, juke stats, and game the system—was cleverly portrayed in the HBO series *The Wire*. Thanks to claims about their wild success by Bratton and Rudy Giuliani (New York's mayor at the time), programs like CompStat were soon exported to other cities worldwide.[34]

Their spread laid the groundwork for the future of data-driven policing.

The latest phase of smart policing seeks to move the temporal focus forward even further, from reactive and proactive to *predictive* policing. A direct extension of previous strategies, predictive policing applies the power of data-driven analytics and statistical models to tell officers where crime is likely to happen, and who is likely to commit it.[35]

The company PredPol, founded in 2012 with the help of Bratton after he moved from New York City to be the police chief of the LAPD, was a pioneer in modern predictive policing. "PredPol uses a proprietary algorithm predicated on the near-repeat model, which suggests once a crime occurs in a location, the immediate surrounding area is at increased risk for subsequent crime," writes Brayne.[36] The algorithm is fed three types of data about past crime: the type of crime, the place it occurred, and at what time. From that data, PredPol predicts what parts of the city have a high risk of crime so that police can focus their attention in those areas.

To give you an idea of how fast this current phase of smart policing is developing, even though it was founded less than a decade ago, PredPol's algorithm is fairly simplistic compared to the surveillance systems and predictive models that some police departments are now deploying. For example, a predictive tool called HunchLab "primarily surveys past crimes, but also digs into dozens of other factors like population density; census data; the locations of bars, churches, schools, and transportation hubs; schedules for home games—even moon phases," the Verge reports.[37] The drive to collect all the data possible—essentially, no matter how seemingly irrelevant or intrusive—and hope it pays off later has become part of how cities are policed. By now this might not be a surprising discovery, but that doesn't mean the impacts and implications are any less important, or even shocking.

Consider a particularly controversial illustration. In an attempt to further hone their analysis—and fully embrace the creepiness of big data policing—officers in the Chicago Police Department preemptively visited residents that were on a computer-generated heat list, which marked them as likely to be involved in a future violent crime.[38] These people had done nothing wrong, but the Chicago Police Department wanted to let them know that officers would be keeping tabs on them. In effect, they were already considered suspects for crimes not yet committed.

By continuously collecting and crunching data, a host of companies like PredPol and HunchLab aim to equip police with analytics that can tell them how as well as where to deploy resources in the most efficient, effective ways. The quest for more accurate predictions has led to more surveillance that feeds more data into more complex algorithms. It's a vicious cycle that justifies the nonstop amplification of police powers.

Of course, not even big data can actually tell the future. The clairvoyants in *Minority Report* are still science fiction. In reality, predictive policing is just a gamble on probability: the chance that some crime will happen in some place, perhaps by some specific person. That hardly matters when the true power of analytics does not necessarily come from evidence of their accuracy but rather a belief in their authority.[39]

Information Automation

The third shift is in how police find and track information: from query-based searches to automated alerts. If you have seen a police procedural like *Law & Order* or *CSI*, then you have seen officers and detectives search for information in specialized databases. They can, for instance, run a license plate to see who owns a vehicle or search a data bank for matches to a fingerprint. The police have access to many databases that contain information not generally (or easily) available to the public. Yet getting that information required actively searching for it by submitting a request and sifting through the results. This could take a great deal of time and it often required already having some idea of what information you wanted. Once the information was retrieved, its significance might not be readily apparent, so the detectives and technicians had to analyze the data, find patterns, and connect the dots. It's easy to see how cop shows can squeeze so many hours of television out of this process.

Now, however, the police are taking the mantra of "work smarter, not harder" to heart. Rather than actively searching and parsing through information, the police can actively feed data into systems, and then wait for the software to tell them what it means or when something happens. These automated systems make continuous data collection a core part of the police's job. "Soon it will be feasible and affordable for the government to record, store and analyze nearly everything we do," writes law professor Elizabeth Joh. "The police will rely on alerts generated by computer programs that sift through the massive quantities of available information for patterns of suspicious activity."[40]

While queries are still very much central to police investigations, the trajectory here (as in many other sectors) is headed toward more automation. A recent Chinese state propaganda film called *Amazing China* perfectly encapsulates this shift: "'If there are anomalies, the system sends an alert,' a narrator says, as Chinese police officers pay a visit to an apartment with a record of erratic electricity use. The film then quotes one of the officers: 'No matter which corner you escape to, we'll bring you to justice.'"[41] Whereas the Chinese police are explicit about their technological capabilities—even to the point of putting on demonstrations for journalists—the North Americans prefer to keep the extent of their power under wraps.

Moreover, these systems make it much easier for the police to conduct surveillance. Let's say an officer wants to keep a close watch on a specific person's activities. Now the officer simply has to set up an alert in the database, which will then notify the officer anytime new information about the person is inputted into the system. If an automatic license plate reader (ALPR)—a camera equipped with software that captures the location and time of all vehicle licenses it sees—mounted on a light pole records the person's car existing or leaving a specific geofenced area, *ding!* The officer gets a notification in real time on their phone. Or if the person is randomly stopped on the street by another cop, who then files a standard report about the interaction, *ding!* The officer can read that report. This type of targeted tracking and real-time alerts can also be set up for specific addresses and areas.

The work of watching people and places is another job that's being automated by companies like Palantir, the military intelligence turned social surveillance firm. If we made *Law & Order: Smart Policing Unit*, multiple episodes would just revolve around our intrepid detectives doing data entry, justifying the decision to track somebody, and waiting for software to alert them of suspicious activity.

Data Dragnet

The fourth shift is the lowering of thresholds for being included in police databases. We expect there to be a record of people who have had direct encounters with the police and courts, whether that means being arrested and "booked," being fined for a minor infraction, or calling to report an emergency. We also expect the police to collect progressively more information, like mugshots and fingerprints, when somebody has been taken into custody for a crime. Most people would likely see this as a reasonable practice of information gathering and file keeping. At the same time, most people would likely be outraged if the police started taking DNA samples, fingerprints, and mugshots from every random person they came across.

This is because we have a sense that certain criteria should be met for police to collect certain types of data, from certain people, for certain purposes. These criteria, or thresholds for inclusion, set important limits on police to ensure they act in ways that truly "protect and serve" the public. Ideally, in a democratic society, the public's expected threshold and the police's enacted threshold are in alignment.

Yet the rise of smart policing has spurred a rapid decline in the thresholds for inclusion into police databases. Thanks to new capacities to analyze data and new imperatives to extract it, "the police increasingly utilize data on individuals who have not had any police contact at all," Brayne explains. "Quotidian activities are being codified by law enforcement organizations."[42] All the cars driving past an ALPR camera are stored in a police database. All the phones that connect to a StingRay device are logged by a police database. All the people, vehicles, addresses, and phone numbers that are somehow connected to a "person of interest" are on the police's radar.

Critics argue that businesses and governments should both adhere to the principle of *data minimization*: only collecting, storing, and analyzing the data needed for a specific purpose.

But devices like ALPRs and data analytics like Palantir do exactly the opposite by capturing everything and everybody.

Instead, these organizations are driven by a principle of *data maximization*: recording and storing all data, from all sources, by any means possible, even if its use is not yet apparent. Restricting data collection is "largely antithetical to the rationale of big data and the functioning of data markets which seek to generate and hoard large volumes of data to extract additional value," argues Rob Kitchin, a scholar of smart cities.[43]

The detrimental impacts of mass surveillance have been well documented.[44] It has chilling effects on people's behavior. It sacrifices civil liberties for the promise of security. It criminalizes everyday life by casting suspicion on even mundane activities. It undermines the very legitimacy and accountability required for a functioning democracy. When Edward Snowden raised alarms about the warrantless, dragnet surveillance of the NSA, little did we know that cities had their own mini-NSAs in the form of police departments. Unlike the NSA, however, the police are also in regular, intimate contact with the communities they surveil—with the power to harass, arrest, deport, and even kill their targets.

Max Fusion

The fifth shift is the integration of data from different sources into massive, centralized, searchable databases. In addition to collecting new data due to lower inclusion thresholds, the police are accessing and combining data held by various institutions—both public and private—that was previously kept separated, and might have been off-limits to the police.

This is part of a widespread practice called "data fusion": the sharing and merging of data from multiple sources to reveal new information, patterns, and correlations, which can then enhance the accuracy of profiles and predictions. Data fusion is a powerful technique because it can uncover private information and circumvent data security. With data fusion, it's possible to discover personal details about somebody—such as their sexuality, political ideology, health conditions, or home address—without having direct access to that information. In other words, data fusion is a way of breaking down the firewalls between different databases, possibly revealing sensitive information that should not be (easily) accessed by governments and/or corporations.

The shift toward data fusion in policing has been supported by infrastructure and funding from the Department of Homeland Security. According to the surveillance researchers Torin Monahan and Priscilla Regan, Homeland Security has created "a robust network of 'fusion centers' to disseminate and analyze data on suspicious individuals or activities, assist with investigations, and identify potential threats." There are at least seventy-seven such fusion centers, not including the "many unofficial public- and private-sector intelligence analysis organizations that perform similar functions."[45] In order to operate, fusion centers also rely on specially designed hardware and software from tech corporations like IBM's i2 Coplink and Microsoft's Fusion Core.

These fusion centers are treated like a "one-stop shop" where police and federal agencies can access and analyze a staggering amount of data drawn from many different sources.[46] The extent of the fusion centers' capabilities are unknown since, due to the nature of their work, the Department of Homeland Security and police are secretive about their operations.[47] What is clear, though, is that the scope of fusion centers has quickly expanded from an initial focus on "counterterrorism" to general application for "all crimes."[48] This mission creep is predictable. Smart systems of surveillance and control are justified for specific purposes, but once they are put into action they are widely used for other reasons—both legal and illegal. Yet it can be hard to keep track of the creep, since the watchers resist being watched.

Data fusion also means that many institutions now act like eyes and ears for the police, which diminishes the rights and deters the behavior of people who rely on those institutions but don't trust the police. For example, according to a sociological study, individuals who have come in contact with the police tend to avoid other "surveilling institutions" that might provide information to the police, such as hospitals, schools, banks, and welfare agencies.[49] Thus even just by enacting constant and expansive surveillance, the police deter people from accessing the services they deserve and need.

With policing based on the principle of data maximization, all data is now potentially police data.

The Captured City

Together, as forces of amplification and transformation, these five major shifts in smart policing have set in motion radical changes in urban governance. In addition to targeting people and populations, the police are now analyzing profiles and patterns. The subjects of surveillance are no longer merely humans but rather the data streams that stand in for humans. This is what Deleuze called the dividual: a person who is sliced and segmented into data, and then surveilled and scrutinized by analytics. Dividuals are easier to administer than individuals. They fit better into databases and processors. They can be atomized and spread across different databases, only to be reassembled later by "various authorities seeking to discipline the behavior of individuals" who somehow run afoul of the system, crossing the line between freedom and oppression.[50]

In short, smart policing has catalyzed the creation of totalizing systems that aim to capture the entire city by sucking everything into their databases and subjecting everybody to their power—all the better to create profiles, calculate patterns, and control people.

Rather than imagining utopian visions of a shining city on the hill, when we think of the real smart city we should think of things like the Domain Awareness System (DAS): a joint venture between the NYPD and Microsoft, which the NYPD claims is "one of the world's largest networks" of urban surveillance.[51]

The DAS connects together New York's vast infrastructure of cameras and sensors, and "applies massive processing power to rapidly sort through NYC's surveillance data," explains Josh Scannell, a sociologist who has done extensive research on the NYPD's use of data-driven tech.[52] Officers equipped with smartphones and tablets have mobile, real-time access to the DAS. This gives them the ability to do things like pull up feeds from CCTV cameras, search a range of databases that are integrated into the DAS, and set up automatic alerts for when the DAS detects "suspicious activity."

The DAS, Scannell writes, is another product of the global "war on terror"; when the enemy can be anywhere, the battlespace is everywhere:

> Built with Homeland Security funds under an antiterrorism mandate, its surveillance extends far beyond the obviously "criminal" to include data as exotic as feeds from radiation detectors—sensitive enough to pick up recent chemotherapy treatment in passing bodies—and sophisticated enough to rapidly recall up to five years'

worth of stored "metadata" and temporally unbounded (and unde-
fined) "environmental data" in its continuously mined databases.[53]

The DAS integrates the five shifts outlined above into the
ultimate, unified smart platform, which contributes to creating
what I call the *captured city*. It is captured in two ways: by corporate and military surveillance systems that aspire to always
watch everything, and by police who occupy and control urban
space. The captured city is the result of public-private partnerships, which compound the worst excesses of both forms of
power.

Other cities around the world have looked at the DAS—and
similar types of control centers and analytics platforms built by
corporations like IBM and Cisco—as models for how to govern
urban society.[54] As the tech advances, increasingly more powerful hardware and software can be built on and integrated into
these platforms. The city provides infinite possibilities for smart
upgrades.

Upgrades already on the market include hardware supplied
by the ominously named company Persistent Surveillance Systems. The tech, originally created for use by the US military in
Iraq before being sold as a service to police departments, consists
of a small airplane equipped with an array of high-resolution
cameras. By flying in orbit over the city, "the plane's wide-
angle cameras captured an area of roughly 30 square miles and
continuously transmitted real-time images to analysts on the
ground," according to an investigation by Bloomberg Businessweek.[55] The plane can fly for six to eight hours before needing
to refuel, allowing it to watch the city without interruption for
long periods.

Persistent Surveillance Systems blankets the city from above,
while other hardware aims to capture the city from the street

level. One of the most scandalous examples of these corporate-police partnerships is the rapid rollout of Amazon's Ring, a smart doorbell with a camera that records and stores video. Through secretive agreements with Ring, police departments in dozens of cities across the United States have partnered with the company to supply discounted or free devices to citizens, "sometimes using taxpayer funds to pay for Amazon's products," reports CNET. Citizens get a cool new device for their front door, and in return Amazon profits from data storage fees and police have a distributed network of cheap cameras that they can access through a "law enforcement dashboard" provided by Ring and connected to its app Neighbors. As reporter Alfred Ng remarks, "While residential neighborhoods aren't usually lined with security cameras, the smart doorbell's popularity has essentially created private surveillance networks powered by Amazon and promoted by police departments."[56] By selling (or giving away) these devices as consumer goods, typically through fear-based marketing, Amazon and police can avoid public oversight of how these cameras proliferate, how their video data is used, and why police can request or even mandate access to this system of street surveillance.

On the software front, applications powered by facial recognition and artificial intelligence have become widely available, allowing police to integrate them into already-existing CCTV cameras and officer body cameras. Now every cop on patrol can be equipped with a mobile, real-time facial recognition scanner—like is already happening in China.[57] What's more, along with services like Amazon's Rekognition—Amazon truly is the vanguard of our brave new digital capitalist hellscape—other tech companies are developing artificial-intelligence-powered systems marketed as "Google for CCTV," which enable users to search through video footage with keywords.[58] Rather than manually skimming through countless hours of video to find, say, a man wearing a red shirt or driving a certain model of car, police can simply enter their query and find all the relevant clips.

When taken together, this hardware and software seeks to leave no moment in the captured city unrecorded, unanalyzed, and unsearchable.

It's difficult to overstate how much power the integration of software like facial recognition and hardware like aerial surveillance grants to police departments and government agencies. Just consider for a second having the ability to monitor, passively and constantly, people and places. Even setting aside the intolerable potential for abuse, the "normal use" of these systems is a serious threat to democratic rights.

All the while, tech corporations turn a profit by selling the advanced tools that are used to invade privacy, target people, and violate civil liberties, or by wielding those tools themselves to extract even more data and profit.[59] Smart policing and the captured city are good business for Silicon Valley.

The frightening reality is that no matter how benevolent or well intentioned their users are, these systems contribute to one ultimate goal: the total domination of urban space-time. As a textbook on "intelligence gathering and crime analysis" puts it, "If knowledge is power, then foreknowledge can be seen as battlespace dominance or supremacy."[60] This is what the militarization of policing and public space looks like in the digital age.

The logic of the captured city is that with enough ubiquitous surveillance and processing power, the totality of the city—every place, every moment—can be made knowable and controllable over time. The explicit goal of these technologies' creators and users is to acquire the power to press rewind on the city, pause it at any point, and watch it unfold over time, or hit fast-forward and devise predictive models that inform anticipatory policing and planning. Any person or place is made available for real-time tracking; all profiles and patterns are revealed through data-driven analysis. Instead of navigating the messiness of a chaotic system, they can impose order on a captured city.

Secret Police

Perhaps one of the most insidious aspects of this supercharged level of surveillance and control in our cities is that its systems are frequently invisible. The watchers, sensors, trackers, interceptors, gatekeepers, and networks tying them all together are the hidden infrastructure of urban places. They are designed to blend into the background and go unnoticed. If you know what you're looking for, perhaps you can spot the signs of the smart city.[61] You can find the clusters of cameras and sensors strapped to light poles, where the city is monitored and recorded. You can stand on the sidewalk in front of buildings that house data centers and control rooms, where the city is stored and analyzed.

Even then, this will only give you a glimpse of smart urbanism in action. It is difficult to investigate or criticize something that is hidden from view or only revealed in flashes. The invisibility is not just because they are digital—we can't physically touch data streams and network connections; more important, the very existence of these systems is intentionally concealed from the public.

This covert style of operation shields smart policing from scrutiny. As a report from Human Rights Watch explains, law enforcement deploys an evolving array of invasive, and even illegal, tactics without being held accountable for civil rights violations, wrongful prosecution, systemic bias, and other abuses of power.[62]

Even if political and public pressure tried to force police to explain how, for example, the predictive algorithms and risk scores they use actually work, they likely would not be able to do so. Since much of the smart tech for police is built by for-profit companies, the way they are designed and operate is proprietary. This means the tech is not open to inspection by the police and judges who use them, let alone oversight by the public. What data are they using? How are they weighing variables? What values and biases are coded into them? In fact, the very companies that develop the algorithms might be unable answer all those questions due to the technical complexity of machine learning.[63] And the things they do know won't be divulged anyway because they are legally protected trade secrets.

When police say they are using data-driven techniques to make smarter decisions, too often what they really mean is they are using software that spits out numbers and models, without any real understanding of how, why, or what it means. It seems that smart policing requires a tremendous faith in the veracity of analytics and their programmers, or at least a willingness to trade knowledge and accountability for the promise of data and power.

Even with a limited ability to audit these systems, study after study shows that techniques like predictive policing are highly susceptible to feedback loops that act as justification for the status quo and encode biases that target marginalized populations, all while having questionable effects on crime rates.[64] It's simple: if police arrest relatively more people from a certain social group or neighborhood, then the predictive model will tell them to spend more time watching those people and places, and that means even more arrests. This vicious cycle further replicates existing practices like racial profiling, but now grants them a data-driven justification.[65]

The journalists Ali Winston and Ingrid Burrington have called this a form of "tech-washing for racially biased, ineffective policing methods."[66] Rather than serving as neutral arbiters of fairness and punishment, these algorithms easily become ways of laundering both subjective values and structural biases into ostensibly objective judgments. Prediction gives way to self-fulfilling prophecy.

Yet these stark problems have not stopped the spread of smart tech in police departments worldwide. Faced with sharp criticisms and negative outcomes, police regularly double down on their use of surveillance and analytics as a necessary strategy for policing in the twenty-first century. To be sure, data analytics can be used to great effect, potentially enhancing the ability of police to make more informed, less biased decisions about law enforcement. But the enthusiastic and rapid adoption of smart tech has happened at the expense of meaningful public input, safeguards against misconduct, and other basic procedures of accountability. The contemporary culture and track record of policing does little to assuage any worries. If anything, those factors should deepen our concern about how smart tech is used, for what ends, and to whose detriment, especially when so much of this tech—like the "threat scores" and heat lists—further encourages officers to view entire swaths of the population as dangerous threats. The presumption is that these people are already criminals who just haven't been captured yet.

Taken to its logical conclusion, the shift toward police secretly deploying powerful forms of data collection and social control is also a process of the police claiming ultimate authority over cities and their inhabitants. This means much more than enforcing the laws of their jurisdiction.

- It means ruling over territories and populations through "the administration of bodies and the calculated management of life," as Foucault wrote.[67]
- It means sacrificing civil liberty and human life on the altar of security.
- It means foregoing democratic legitimacy for the sake of secrecy.
- It means subverting oversight by local politicians and the public.
- It means rapidly pacifying protests that even just symbolically threaten state authority, commercial property, or capital circulation.
- It means securitizing space and disenfranchising citizens in the name of urban revitalization.
- It means aspiring to possess omniscience and omnipotence over their domain.
- It means constructing an urban war machine that converts the city into a battlespace, the public into either subjects or adversaries, and the enforcement of law and order into an arms race for surveillance and control.

The urban war machine changes the very nature of society, degrading aspects that are essential to a healthy body politic. Prosocial feelings like *trust* become casualties of a smart society. The result is a self-reinforcing sense of alienation and passivity in citizens who live under the watchful eye and iron fist of the captured city. As the Invisible Committee, a French collective of intellectuals, has argued, "We're not experiencing a 'crisis of trust' but the *end* of trust, which has become superfluous to government. Where control and transparency reign, where the subjects' behavior is anticipated in real time through the algorithmic processing of a mass of available data about them, there's no more need to trust them or for them to trust. It's sufficient that they be sufficiently monitored. As [Vladimir] Lenin said, 'Trust is good, control is better.'"[68]

This is a dire warning, and as with any dire warning, it is easy to dismiss so long as it is only a prognosis about what to expect rather than a diagnosis of what has already arrived. Indeed, for many people—who tend to be white and affluent—the captured city probably does not yet feel like a real thing. Our cities don't tangibly feel much different, not any more secure or stifling, than they did before. This is no accident. In addition to being unseen when viewed from the street level, smart policing goes unnoticed in the lives of those who are deemed *good citizens*. Crucially, *they are still caught* in the dragnet of ALPRs, StingRays, aerial surveillance, facial recognition, data fusion centers, and so on. But their neighborhoods are not labeled hot spots and flooded with patrolling cruisers. They are not put on heat lists and intimidated with preemptive warnings. They are not subjected to regular harassment as well as automatic alerts that keep tabs on their routines, movements, and relationships.

If they were targeted by the same aggressive policing as the poor and people of color—if they experienced sociotechnical violence in the same way as the vulnerable and marginalized—then there would likely be much stricter limits on police power. Or at the very least, there might be more critical attention paid to the alarming way in which smart urbanism is being driven by the police-industrial complex.

The targets and consequences of policing, smart or otherwise, will always be uneven. At the same time, it is a delusion of privilege to think that the impacts of smart policing will only ever be felt by other parts of society. The plight of vulnerable communities is intimately tied to the fate of society. They are the testing grounds for new methods of surveillance and control, which are piloted and perfected where the stakes are low, and accountability is nonexistent, before being modified and rolled out as the new normal for everybody else. The version of the smart city described in this chapter shows how the insidious process of mission creep is already well underway.

It's no longer a question of if smart tech is being used—by tech companies, data brokers, bosses, insurers, police, and other powerful interests—to extract data and exercise control. It's now a question of how exactly they will decide to use those capabilities, who they will target, and what will be the consequences. If we don't confront the problems of covert operations and inscrutable authority, then the answer to those critical questions may never be fully known.

III Smart for the People

8 Seizing Smartness: Or, Tactics for a Dumber World

We live in capitalism. Its power seems inescapable. So did the divine right of kings. Any human power can be resisted and changed by human beings.

–Ursula K. Le Guin, "Books Aren't Just Commodities," 2014

Design is the process by which the politics of one world become the constraints on another.

—Fred Turner, "Don't Be Evil," 2017

The smart society is founded on a simplistic sales pitch: in return for integrating a vast array of data-driven, network-connected, automated tech in our lives, we are offered a number of new upgrades and capabilities at every scale.

The smart self promises to achieve the Socratic quest of knowing thyself without the hassle of regular reflection and critical inquiry. We can outsource those tasks to real-time analysis of constantly recorded data, which plots and ranks our progress on the path to human flourishing.

The smart home promises to deliver each of us a personalized palace of convenience, a veritable cocoon of connectivity. Our most intimate spaces will be transformed into superattentive, active environments that respond to our commands, observe our behavioral patterns, and adjust (to) our preferences.

The smart city promises to overhaul our outdated urban centers so that services are optimized and spaces are securitized. By applying this cybernetic model of civics, the complexity and even chaos of cities can finally be brought to order.

In previous work, I have called this process "selling smartness" because the point is to convince us that these systems—and by extension, the visions and values they materialize—are more than good; they are necessary.[1] As we should expect, their pitches emphasize the benefits and elide any problems. Their tone implies we would be fools not to buy now. And I mean, what could be wrong with more convenience and efficiency?

Perhaps we could tolerate the stale rhetoric about Silicon Valley saving the world if these promised benefits were delivered without any strings attached or surprise consequences. But of course we know things are not so simple. For every smart self-tracker, there are data brokers and bosses who see new tools to exploit people. For every smart home appliance, there are manufacturers and insurers that see new opportunities to extract value. For every smart city solution, there are police departments and platforms that see new methods to exercise authority.

The influence of power and profit, collection and control, corrupts these technological transformations at their source. As society is updated and retrofitted according to the needs of digital capitalism, things are getting too smart for our own good.

For a New Paradigm

Rather than trying to rehabilitate and appropriate the label, there is good reason to disavow *smart* as a paradigm. It's certainly true that *not all* smart things contribute to nefarious ends; there are many useful smart things that enhance life. But we have also seen how smart tech, even when designed for totally innocuous reasons, easily plugs into existing networks of monitoring, managing, manipulating, and monetizing people. Not always, and not to the same degree, yet the examples are legion enough to warrant critical concern.

This isn't necessarily just because these things are made by myopic engineers or greedy companies (although that does contribute to the problem). It is instead a symptom of the social, political, and economic conditions that smart tech emerges from. In his foundational article "Do Artifacts Have Politics?" Langdon Winner explained how this dynamic contributes to technological development and outcomes:

> Indeed, many of the most important examples of technologies that have political consequences are those that transcend the simple categories of "intended" and "unintended" altogether. These are instances in which the very process of technical development is so thoroughly biased in a particular direction that it regularly produces results counted as wonderful breakthroughs by some social interests and crushing setbacks by others. In such cases it is neither correct nor insightful to say, "Someone intended to do somebody else harm." Rather, one must say that the technological deck has been stacked long in advance to favor certain social interests, and that some people were bound to receive a better hand than others.[2]

Whether criticizing or proposing alternatives, Winner shows us why it is important not to become so distracted by *the technology*—as if it exists outside social contexts and human decisions—that we ignore the broader conditions of its creation. In the case of smart tech, I have argued that it is the progeny of technocratic and capitalist parents. Their characteristics are encoded into its design. It has been conditioned to further the aims of data collection and social control. There are surely examples of smart tech that counter this claim. My point here, however, is about the general trends and trajectories of digital capitalism. Exceptions to the rule don't negate the rule. By now there should be little doubt about smart tech's utility as a means to enrich and empower capital.

At the same time, there's no doubt that digital innovations can be designed and used for other purposes. Modifying and repurposing existing tech is *necessary*, but it is not *sufficient* to challenge the imperatives and interests I have mapped out. If we limit ourselves to tinkering at the edges—if we focus on changing technology, while maintaining the same technopolitics—then we hamstring our capacity for change.

Designing a different kind of society based on different kinds of tech will require radical change that threatens the position of the powerful and privileged. But first we have to overcome our own mental blockages. "In the present climate, around the world, almost everything that can be proposed as an alternative will appear to be either utopian or trivial. Thus, our programmatic thinking is paralyzed," observed Roberto Unger, a philosopher and Brazilian politician.[3] If Silicon Valley can build an empire out of trivial proposals dressed up as utopian promises, then we should feel free to brainstorm our own ideas for revolution. Anytime somebody belittles criticism for not being constructive or dismisses demands for not being detailed blueprints, that's just another case of the status quo sapping radical energy.

In an effort to jump-start more of the positive, programmatic work needed to create a different society, I offer a framework based on three forms of collective action, which aim to confront and change digital capitalism. There is plenty of room for this framework to grow and morph to include a diversity of other tactics.

The first starts with acts of everyday resistance and then argues for unmaking certain technical systems. The second begins with the need for democratic technopolitics and then provides a model for taking control of innovation. The third starts with protection from data abuses and then proposes treating data as a public asset for the common good.

Deconstructing Capital

In the twenty-first-century grocery store, employees called pickers are in charge of "walking the aisles of the supermarket—selecting items for eight different orders at a time and storing them in assigned boxes in a cart, a single step in the delivery of an online order," according to Adam Barr, who worked as a picker for the large UK grocery chain Sainsbury's. Like the Amazon warehouse workers discussed earlier, pickers are equipped with a handheld electronic device and unique log-in number. The devices direct the pickers from task to task, minute by minute; their "productivity is tracked over time and flagged at weekly evaluations," explains Barr. When pickers fail to meet the stringent performance targets—as regularly happens because people work like humans not robots—the weekly evaluations turn into "ritualistic humiliation."[4]

The workplace is defined by a lack of autonomy and privacy in a way that's unlike almost any other social relationship in most people's lives—setting aside those in prison or grade school.[5] Yet even in this exploitative ecosystem, workers still find ways to push back and reclaim some autonomy through acts of "microresistance." Barr describes a few different ways that pickers, for example, loosen the grip of algorithmic bosses and make "their job more bearable." These include staying logged in to the handset during lunch breaks so that the "average weekly pic rate plummets," causing the algorithm to set a lower target. Or leaving the device "slightly out of its charging station at the end of his shift so that it would run out of charge a few hours into the next shift," thus securing a five- or ten-minute break during the next shift while the manager found a replacement handset.[6] In such cases, it is better to be reprimanded for "human error" than to fully submit to the yoke of algorithmic supervision.

These acts of microresistance may seem insignificant, but each one can have a meaningful effect on individual morale, and collectively they can sway the value proposition of new tech. If workers are busy devising ways of gaming the system rather than succumbing to profit maximization, then the investment for employers may not be worthwhile.

Microresistance highlights a dynamic at the heart of capitalism's evolution, from the Industrial Revolution to the smart society: Finding ways to squeeze more value from workers is a powerful motivation for innovation. In response, workers have always searched for ways to slow down the pace of work, reclaim some of the value they produce, and exercise their human agency. For instance, in 1917 Elizabeth Gurley Flynn, a labor leader with the Industrial Workers of the World and founding member of the American Civil Liberties Union, published a pamphlet called *Sabotage: The Conscious Withdrawal of the Workers' Industrial Efficiency*. "Sabotage means either to slacken up and interfere with the quantity, or to botch in your skill and interfere with the quality, of capitalist production or to give poor service," wrote Flynn.[7] This perfectly describes how workers like Barr, a century later, found ways to disrupt the tyranny of efficiency as enforced by their handheld managers.

Adding grit to an exploitative system designed to be frictionless is good practice. I argue that resisting the machinery of digital capitalism must take seriously the tradition of tactical sabotage. We can find inspiration in the mythical saboteurs of industrial capitalism: the Luddites.

Today the name "Luddite" is only used as an insult, as a way to tarnish people as antitechnology, antiprogress, and backward. Among the tech evangelists and boosterism of Silicon Valley, anybody who is skeptical or critical of technology is instantly deemed a Luddite, and hence dismissed outright. This contemporary usage, though, majorly botches the real history of Luddism and doesn't give actual Luddites nearly enough credit.

The original Luddites were a group of workers in nineteenth-century England that under the cover of darkness, smashed machines in industrial factories (specifically, equipment used to manufacture textiles).[8] The modern usage of Luddite has this much correct—but that's about all it gets right. Luddites weren't motivated by a primitive fear of progress or worry about competition from technological advances. Instead of indiscriminately swinging their sledgehammers, Luddites were intentional about *which* machines they smashed. "The Luddites destroyed frames owned by the manufacturers who doled out substandard wages or paid in goods rather than currency," Robert Byrne notes in his history of Luddism. "Within the same room, machines were smashed or spared according to the business practices of their owners."[9]

Luddism was motivated by factory owners using machines to drastically increase productivity targets, accelerate the pace of work, and squeeze more value from workers. Sound familiar?

"Luddism wasn't a war on machines," writes Byrne.[10] It was a working-class movement, which understood the importance of confronting the technopolitics of industrial capitalism.

By smashing machines, Luddites were targeting the tech that made their lives more miserable, and the engineers and owners who held power over them. The machines are the "material foundation" for the capitalist system of exploitation and extraction. Therefore, dismantling the machinery of capital is also an attempt to challenge the "form of society which utilizes those instruments," as Marx explained.[11] Naturally the bosses who owned the factories and machinery hated the Luddites, just as they still despise any movement by labor that challenges their authority and makes demands for better working conditions. Capital has always relied on militant tactics for subjugating labor and pursuing profit, while also using the courts of law and public opinion to strip labor of any potential to fight back. So the owners imprisoned and defamed the Luddites by making themselves out to be innocent victims of wanton destruction by a group of ignorant, violent thugs. By continuing to use Luddite as a crude insult, we perpetuate this dynamic—and side with the interests of capital.

Rather than look down on Luddism, we should expand on its tactical focus. The struggle against capital is not only limited to workers fighting exploitation at their jobs. If the power of capitalism does not restrain its reach, then why should we restrict our resistance?

Let me be clear: I'm not advising people to arm themselves with sledgehammers, and begin vandalizing and destroying stuff. In addition to being dangerous and risky in many ways, it is not a strategically effective approach. What we need is a more systematic, more intentional type of Luddism—as opposed to the rash vigilante type—that focuses on literally deconstructing digital capitalism. In other words, recalling our discussion of technology as legislation in the first chapter, we need a Luddism as policy.[12]

There is an impulse to constantly build new stuff, more layers of things and systems, tacked onto and piled on top of the current strata. We surely need *alternative* tech, but we also need to *unmake* so much of the tech that already exists.

It is not enough to look around at the world and imagine countless possibilities for constructing, shaping, and interpreting things differently. We have to recognize the materiality of things too—the way they become stable and block change.[13] You can only get so far by ignoring or building around concrete stuff. Eventually those things must be taken apart, cleared away, and unmade in order to open new paths forward. The model of the unmaker was perfectly sketched by philosopher Walter Benjamin in a 1931 essay on "the destructive character." (While Benjamin uses "he," the destructive character has no gender; all people can and should embody the unmaker).

> The destructive character sees nothing permanent. But for this very reason he sees ways everywhere. Where others encounter walls or mountains, there, too, he sees a way. But because he sees a way everywhere, he has to clear things from it everywhere. Not always by brute force; sometimes by the most refined. Because he sees ways everywhere, he always stands at a crossroads. No moment can know what the next will bring. What exists he reduces to rubble—not for the sake of rubble, but for that of the way leading through it.[14]

Unmaking sounds radical, but is it any more radical or ridiculous than turning innovation into a fetish, driven by the incessant need to do something, anything, for the sake of doing it, even if it isn't really all that novel or useful, and then equating

it to social progress? We train people to be innovators, not maintainers, let alone unmakers. Innovation is sexy, maintenance is
boring, and unmaking is deviant.[15]

What do we get from all this innovation? We mostly end
up with an overabundance of solutions looking for problems.
Not all things are created equally, and many things should have
never been created in the first place. At the very least, we cannot take for granted the knee-jerk celebration of making and
damnation of unmaking. If capitalism gets to celebrate "creative
destruction" for its own ends, then why can't we reclaim it for
different ends?

Just opening ourselves to the *possibility of unmaking* helps us
reassess the worth of things in our lives and society. When it
comes to smart tech, we can start unmaking by simply down-
grading the unnecessarily upgraded things that now fill our
lives, homes, and cities. Not everything has to be equipped with
sensors and connected to the cloud. Indeed, most things should
not be. Strip out the sensors! Switch off the signals! Think of it as
Marie Kondo, but for technopolitics. Does this thing contribute
to human well-being and/or social welfare? If not, toss it away!

It's understandable why manufacturers would want to make
things that record real-time information and check-in with corporate servers. But as users, we should learn to embrace what
Jay Stanley, a tech policy analyst at the American Civil Liberties
Union, calls "the virtues of dumbness."[16] This isn't a primitiv-
ist call to go back to using typewriters and telegraphs. Rather,
it's an appeal to think critically about the things we use and
environments we make, and how in return, they use and make
us. Ultimately unmaking means thinking bigger than just down-
grading our smart toasters or detoxing from our smartphones. It

is a method of reckoning with the "material foundations" and "form of society" created by digital capitalism.[17]

On the one hand, the lifestyle gurus in Silicon Valley will happily sell you a disconnected weekend in the woods—like a silent retreat, but with no Wi-Fi signal—so you can briefly escape from the smart society before returning to life as usual. This is a deviously brilliant plan, which convinces people that the solution to the problems of a smart society is paying for the privilege of recharging our physical/mental/spiritual batteries just so we can dive back into the capitalist hellscape, ready to grind harder and produce more. On the other hand, the neo-Luddite attitude recognizes that we need more than just a temporary reprieve from the speed, supervision, judgment, anxiety, and resentment induced by capitalism. When faced with the decision between adapting to a smarter society or un/making a dumber world, choose the latter.

Of course, we don't have to start immediately with, for example, demolishing the planetary infrastructure of surveillance (though it's good to visualize goals from the beginning). Before taking any direct action, we could go a long way simply by having much higher expectations for how society is organized—and how our lives are shaped—by technopolitical systems. We should not settle for a pittance of marginal upgrades while those in power enjoy major benefits. If we made that one adjustment, and held the design and use of smart tech to new standards, I suspect many of the "innovations" sold as solutions for various problems would not pass muster. Those that don't actually enhance life and benefit society—which instantly excludes nearly all smart tech designed to expand data extraction and social control—should be unmade.

Democratizing Innovation

People will slip through the cracks of a smart society. Sometimes that's a good thing. The goal of blanketing the globe in systems designed to capture everything—remember IBM's slogan "building a smarter planet"—can make it hard to forget that people find ways to avoid, deceive, or subvert even the most totalitarian system.[18] Perhaps people will keep their junk food in a retro dumb fridge to hide it from the prying eyes of insurance companies. Perhaps they will wear special antisurveillance fashion that confuses facial recognition and makes its wearer invisible to artificial-intelligence-powered surveillance.[19] Perhaps they will benefit from a glitch in some scoring system, which boosts their rank and grants access to high-status perks.

Inevitability, people will devise unexpected ways of using smart tech—ways we cannot foresee until necessity stokes ingenuity. Put differently, creators don't hold all the power; users are also "agents of technological change," as historian Ronald Kline and sociologist Trevor Pinch argue in their influential study of how automobile owners modified and reinterpreted vehicles to fit their own needs and desires.[20] Even as we acknowledge the agency of users, however, strategically we cannot rest on the fact, as sci-fi author William Gibson put it, that "the street finds its own uses for things—uses the manufacturers never imagined."[21]

Hoping that enough people will, on their own, discover ways to cope with technological change is doing less than nothing. There is a reason why the idea that people will "muddle through" also supports what one libertarian analyst calls "permissionless innovation."[22] It's another name for corporations, and their think tank surrogates, eliminating organized opposition and regulation.

Relying on ingenious individuals is not a sufficient or sustainable way to combat the injustices of a smart society, let alone take hold of its developmental direction. Doing so also risks underplaying the very real power asymmetries between different groups involved in designing and using tech. (De)constructive tactics for change need to be collective and intentional.[23]

I have discussed why existing things need to be taken apart. So how should we put new things together? By taking control of innovation!

This sounds like an oxymoron: How can anybody control innovation?[24] We've been taught to think about innovation as a result of unexpected ideas and great men, which then produce technoscientific advances that improve human life. This view was most clearly expressed by the chemist and philosopher Michael Polanyi: "You can kill or mutilate the advance of science, you cannot shape it. For it can advance only by essentially unpredictable steps, pursuing problems of its own, and the practical benefits of these advances will be incidental and hence doubly unpredictable."[25] For Polanyi, "innovation" and "the market" were similar in that they should both be free of any human interference. This means no attempts to shape or regulate their processes and outcomes. The only guidance for both innovation and markets, according to this argument, should come from the invisible hand—that is, the spontaneous order of unplanned behavior and individual decisions rather than collective, intentional action.

This story of how innovation happens is based on a convenient mythology. It excludes all but the chosen few from taking part in the process of innovation. It then shields scientists, engineers, and entrepreneurs from any obligations or responsibilities they have for the outcomes of their work.[26] When faced with tough questions, the mysterious dynamics of innovation (or the market) are a handy scapegoat.

Yet far from being an unbridled force of nature, innovation has become big business. Decisions about why, what, and how to make technology are now largely concentrated in the hands of venture capitalists, private companies, and the military, while the rest of us must live with the products of their decisions. At each stage of the process, from investment to implementation, new technologies are subjected to layers of oversight and evaluation. Their development is directed toward certain goals and designed with certain values. If the product is deemed a flop, then it's tossed into the trash heap. If it is a success, then it's sold as an innovation. It's not a question of if there can be protocols for managing innovation but instead who gets to create the protocols?

This disparity in who gets to be included in the innovation process is not only limited to a wealth gap. Studies about who receives funding from venture capitalists show significant patterns of gender and racial discrimination against entrepreneurs.[27] It should go without saying, but this is not because only white men have ideas worth funding. Simply look around at all the start-ups that amass and burn rounds of venture capital just to create new ways of expanding "the Internet of things your mom won't do for you anymore," as the *Harvard Business Review* called it.[28] Meritocracy, in the way that term is used now, is another name for the same people doing the same shit and patting each other on the back for it.

Venture capitalists are not divining rods for innovation. They often prefer to dump their money into the people they perceive as being safe bets. Investment patterns tend to avoid experimenting with subversive ideas. Instead, "smart innovation appears more an exercise of replication via short-term and financially risk-averse projects."[29] In the search for the next "unicorn"—a company valued at $1 billion—venture capitalists tend to follow the "patterns" (read: copying other successes) and listen to their "intuitions" (read: implicit biases). For instance, when Mark Zuckerberg hit the mother lode as a brash Ivy League dropout in a hoodie, suddenly venture capitalists were throwing money at every Zuckerberg look-alike that walked into their offices. The invisible hand of innovation sure appears a lot like maintaining the status quo.

There are more important problems to solve with and more beneficial outcomes to gain from smart tech. Rather than unleashing the true potential of smart tech to improve society for everybody, untold amounts of money, time, and energy are invested—no, wasted—on creating systems that exist on a spectrum from extractive and repressive to irritating and inane. We deserve better than the schlock that Silicon Valley currently specializes in churning out.

When I say we need to take control of innovation, I mean we need to *democratize* innovation by giving more people more power to influence how, why, and for what purpose new technology is created. This means not treating innovation like a mystical force only accessed by an elite class but rather a human endeavor that should benefit everybody. The case is sharply made by political scientist Richard Sclove: "If citizens ought to be empowered to participate in determining their society's basic structure, and technologies are an important species of social structure, it follows that technological design and practice should be democratized."[30]

Democratizing innovation involves two major reforms:

1. Allowing those effected by the use of technology to participate in its creation, thereby including a diverse range of groups

that may have different interests, experiences, and values. Truly participatory design has to go beyond just rebranding public relations as public engagement. This means treating people as more than merely consumers in a marketplace, but instead as citizens with rights to codetermine the systems that shape their lives.[31] Participants must at least have the capacity to provide meaningful feedback and catalyze transformative change that challenges the nature as well as goals of innovation.

2. Opening up the black box of opaque operations and proprietary processes, thus ensuring that intelligent systems are also *intelligible* to the public.[32] Truly intelligible systems have to go beyond companies sharing certain data sets or organizing occasional hackathons where programmers can play around. This also means calling for more than transparency, which is only the first step toward accountability. They must be scrutinized and regulated by independent experts and advocates who work for the public interest, not private benefit.

The case for these changes, and how they can be effectively enacted, has been the subject of much research, writing, and experimentation. My own previous work has contributed to these efforts and detailed their importance.[33] Instead of summarizing this body of work, I want to resurface a largely forgotten event from the past that should serve as an inspiration for the future.[34]

Seizing the Means of Innovation

In 1976, workers at Lucas Aerospace, a major manufacturer in the United Kingdom, decided they were done making weapons for war and profits for capital. "Around half of Lucas Aerospace's output supplied military contracts," explains Adrian Smith, professor of technology policy. "Since this business area depended upon public funds, as did many of the firm's civilian products, workers argued state support [would] be better put to developing more *socially useful products*." Therefore, they crafted the Alternative Corporate Plan—or the Lucas Plan—which "proposed innovative alternatives" for how to manage manufacturing and what to produce.[35]

These were unstable times for the economy. Due to industrial restructuring and capital relocation, workers were facing a massive wave of terminations that threatened their livelihoods. It hardly seemed like the moment to shake things up and risk being fired for challenging factory owners. But the workers at Lucas were energized by the actions of labor movements during that period. They knew there would never be a perfect opportunity to enact radical democratic change. Instead, they recognized that it is always the right time to put into practice ideas about human-centered design and socially useful production.

The Lucas Plan detailed a new movement for technopolitics. Far from being just another utopian manifesto, however, the plan originated as a concrete proposal for saving jobs and stopping factory closures at Lucas Aerospace. It took seriously the question of how to create an innovation system that achieves lofty goals like promoting human progress, enhancing social welfare, and empowering all people in all places, while also meeting immediate needs like ensuring workers had safe, guaranteed, and well-paying jobs to support their families.

Based on a participatory process that used a questionnaire distributed to workers on the factory floor, the Lucas Plan was a detailed report on all aspects of socially useful production. In addition to "designs for over 150 alternative products," Adrian Smith wrote in this report,

> it contained market analyses and economic considerations; proposals for employee training that enhanced and broadened skills; and suggested a restructuring of work organization into less hierarchical teams, breaking divisions between practical shop floor knowledge and theoretical design engineering knowledge. The Plan challenged fundamental assumptions about how innovation and business should be run.[36]

The plan's scope was *not* limited to reforms for a single company. As one of its leaders said, it was meant to "inflame the imaginations of others," and "demonstrate in a very practical and direct way the creative power of 'ordinary people.'"[37] By that measure, the plan was successful. Its implications were widely discussed in the international press at the time. The plan was fertilizer for the growth of a "grassroots innovation movement," as Smith calls it, of "initiatives for socially useful production [that] emerged from the bottom-up, in shop floors, in polytechnics, and in local communities."[38] The UK industry secretary at the time, Tony Benn, called it, "One of the most remarkable exercises that's ever occurred in British industrial history."[39] The Lucas Plan was even nominated for the Nobel Peace Prize in 1979.

By drafting this alternative blueprint, workers at Lucas Aerospace proved that innovation was not a mysterious force that can only be grasped by technocratic high priests. They demonstrated that "ordinary people" are an untapped well of novel ideas and possess the skills needed to organize production for *socially useful outcomes*. We are excluded because it upsets the control that capital wields over labor and profit. It is not a lack of knowledge but instead an act of power that prevents us from democratizing innovation and distributing its fruits to everybody.

The Lucas Plan faced opposition on multiple fronts. It took management at the company years after the plan's launch just to discuss parts of it with worker representatives. The company did that much only after pressure from social movement activity and media coverage. Additionally, the plan had to fight against the rising tide of Thatcherism, which hollowed out labor unions and implemented a brutal economic ideology. The managerial class, military-industrial complex, and neoliberal government all viewed the plan, rightfully so, as a threat to their power. Thus they rejected it outright, even in cases where the alternative products and management structure would have been profitable.[40] Due to such strong opposition, the plan was not implemented at Lucas Aerospace. But its relevance and importance extend much further than this particular time and place.

The plan still serves as a model for practically and systematically trying to change how innovation is done—by the people, for the public. I don't mean model in the sense of copying and pasting it from then to now but rather as an exemplar that should be plucked from the dustbin of history, brushed off, and reexamined for a different age.

The plan's original framers argued that there is an obligation to use public funding to support socially useful production. Their assertion is still valid and relevant today. Almost all the things we associate with innovation—from iPhones and the internet to biotech—were supported by government investment. As economist Mariana Mazzucato expertly details in her book *The Entrepreneurial State*, governments play a major role in funding the research and development that leads to innovation.[41] The problem is that the current model socializes risks and privatizes rewards: governments spend public money and bear the risks of investment, while businesses claim ownership and reap the benefits. Silicon Valley, for example, would basically not exist if not for the long list of technoscientific discoveries funded by government agencies, not to mention the cash injections and business deals that prop up iconic companies like SpaceX and Amazon. Indeed, some of the most exalted entrepreneurs like Elon Musk are, in many respects, glorified government contractors.

Corporate executives declare that government is terrible at picking winners and losers, but they are happy to cash the checks of public investment. So in a sense, they are correct: currently, government is picking the wrong winners—corporate shareholders over public stakeholders. We should be rejecting this model of trickle-down innovation. It's not a question of if public funding can support innovation—all the evidence points to an emphatic "Yes, it does!"—but rather what kind of innovation and for whose benefit.

The time is ripe for a Lucas Plan 2.0, a strategy for building a better technological society—one that is more inclusive, equitable, and empowering for everybody.

What kind of proposals might the next version focus on? Outlining a whole new plan has to be a participatory, grassroots effort. I submit, instead, that the cornerstone of any strategy has to center on reforming the lifeblood of digital capitalism: data.

Demanding Data

In terms of influence and wealth, the data hoarders are already usurping the oil barons and hedge fund managers. "It used to be banks, but now it is tech giants that dominate the US lobbying industry," as journalists Olivia Solon and Sabrina Siddiqui report.[42] The skepticism, protest, and vigilance that has long been focused on Wall Street must now also be directed toward Silicon Valley.

Thanks to a series of scandals and missteps, there has recently been a growing backlash (or "techlash") against the power of the tech sector. The public has begun waking up to the reality that Silicon Valley CEOs—who want to change the world and claim ownership over the future—do not have our best interests at heart. In addition to a rising tide of critical op-eds, employees across the industry are banding together through organizations like the Tech Workers Coalition to demand change in the working conditions and business decisions of large firms like Google.[43] Regulatory agencies like the US Federal Trade Commission have released reports calling for more transparency and accountability in the shadowy data broker industry.[44] Congressional inquiries and newspaper investigations have shown tech giants like Facebook are, at best, deceptive and manipulative stewards of our personal data as well as social relationships.[45] Similarly, Amazon's competition for the location of its new headquarters and Sidewalk Labs' proposed smart city development in Toronto have both been revealing displays of the digital capitalist regime that wields absurd levels of power over (supposedly) sovereign states and cities.[46] In short, these tech giants are proving to be toxic for democracy.

Yet the typical way of framing concerns with smart tech—in terms of privacy, cybersecurity, and attention in an age of unending notifications—severely limits how we understand the problems and search for solutions. In an essay on the history of privacy, Katrina Forrester writes, "Policies to protect privacy appeal to a language of transparency, individual consent, and rights. But they rarely try to disperse the ownership of our data—by breaking the power of monopolies that collect it, or by placing its use under democratic control through public oversight."[47] As I have argued throughout this book, the problems with smart tech are, first and foremost, problems of political economy. And so too must be their solutions.

It seems to me there are two main ways to advance a progressive program for governing data: oversight and ownership. What follows is just an introduction to both approaches, and the beginning of a discussion about how to flesh out these ideas and put them into practice. Ultimately, the first approach should be a stepping-stone to achieve the second.

Demand Oversight

There is an urgent need for strict regulations on what types of data companies can collect, why they collect it, and how much data they can possess, both about individuals and in aggregate. The data banks that centralize immense amounts of valuable data in one place have become too powerful, risky, and big to exist.[48]

The way that the data economy is structured now—with the means of producing, processing, and profiting from data concentrated in the hands of techno-oligarchs—is profoundly damaging to society. To name just a few impacts:

- it accelerates the growth of inequality by providing a new source of power and money that is owned by a few and kept away from the many

- it amplifies the impacts of practices like "digital redlining" that whether intentional or not, harm whole groups of people by empowering predatory behavior and encoding bias into algorithmic actions[49]

- it creates an unstable system that is impossible to secure, as demonstrated by the increasing frequency and severity of data breaches that reveal deeply personal information about astonishing amounts of people

- it resists any attempts to contain the flow of data extracted by one party for one purpose—data that is then sold/given to other parties for other purposes, and is then . . . *ad infinitum*

Data-driven harms are not bugs but rather features of a system where a single flaw or choice can have consequences for countless people and spiral out of control. Each of these core issues needs to be addressed directly.

The data economy could be reformed, in large part, simply by enforcing the laws and regulations that already exist. Many of them were originally written with other industries in mind. They might not address the fundamental causes, but they will lessen the scale and severity of the impacts from big data banks. A few relevant examples include:

- antitrust policy that busted monopolies and punished collusion could be applied to data banks with outsize power in the market
- capital controls that constrain the volatile circulation of financial capital could be applied to data capital to limit where, how, and why data is exchanged
- audits that investigate the operations of businesses to verify their practices are aboveboard could be applied to the ways data is collected, analyzed, and used

Of course these laws need to be modified—and new policies need to be drafted—to fit the context of the data economy. They also need to be updated to reflect a more sophisticated understanding of political economy in the twenty-first century.

For instance, it is not enough to base antitrust on notions of market competition and consumer prices. Doing so allows

Amazon to continue swallowing the whole economy while escaping the antitrust hatchet: since its prices are low, it is deemed to increase "consumer welfare" and thus is left alone.[50] Even a cursory glance at Amazon's expanding economic position and political power shows how inadequate this version of antitrust is for our time. It betrays a myopic view of how exploitation and corruption actually operate in the world. When it comes to the goals and methods for breaking up the data banks, we cannot afford anything less than a clear vision.

Demand Ownership
In the new gilded age, a laissez-faire attitude toward data has encouraged a new gang of robber barons to arise. These corporate executives have enjoyed operating under the freedom of unbridled capitalism—while we have been "free" from adequate protections against the uses and abuses of data—for far too long. Rather than continue allowing them to unscrupulously take, trade, and hoard our data, we must rein in their extractive enterprise and reclaim their ill-gotten gains. Calls for transparency and accountability are a start, but we are way past the point where these tepid responses are sufficient. Protective regulation will alleviate some of the pain, perhaps making things bearable for a while, yet it won't cure the afflictions of digital capitalism. For that we need more serious treatments.

As opposed to tolerating the injustices of data collection for private profit, we should collectivize data for the public good. Data could deliver great benefits for us all—much greater than what the most privileged have enjoyed—but that potential is squandered when data is primarily treated as way of extracting value from and exercising control over the world. Those who could benefit the most from progressive uses of data are too often the people who are exploited and excluded by the current regime of big data. Instead of using data analytics to find people whose lives would be improved by public assistance, for instance, data analytics are used to profile, police, and punish those who are already vulnerable.[51]

The most valuable data—the data coveted by corporations, employers, insurers, police, and so on—comes from people. "Big data, like Soylent Green, is made of people."[52] We might not have shed blood, sweat, and tears to produce that data but nonetheless it is extracted from our bodies, behaviors, preferences, identities, and so forth. Part of us is embedded inside and represented by that data. We are connected to that data and the consequences of its use.

Personal data has become essential to many systems of economic production and social power. It would be foolish and dangerous to go on having no voice in how, why, and for whom they operate. When it comes to these kinds of large-scale, technopolitical systems, philosopher Tony Smith argues that "the principle of democracy must then come into play: all exercises of this authority must be subject to the consent of those impacted by it."[53] Data should be of the people, used for the people, and governed by the people.

How do we make the governance of data more democratic? The answer is to decommodify and collectivize it. In short, decommodify means treating data as more than just a thing that is bought and sold via the market, and only accessed by those who can afford it. Collectivize means managing data as a shared resource—versus only private property—that can contribute to the common good. They are two sides of the same coin.

One possible way of changing governance is by owning and operating the data banks like a public utility. It's like electricity generation and public transportation, but for data infrastructure. "In the past, natural monopolies like utilities and railways that enjoy huge economies of scale and serve the common good have been prime candidates for public ownership," as Nick Srnicek explains in an essay arguing for nationalizing megaplatforms like Google and Facebook.[54]

The point is not for the government to prevent people from gathering data about themselves for their own personal purposes, such as the kind created by wearable trackers or home devices. Instead, the focus here is on large-scale databases that are used for industrial purposes. If anything, collectivizing data would enhance its personal value by ensuring people have access to all the relevant data that is already surreptitiously harvested about them by their devices.

In terms of policy for this shift in data governance, a new public institution—*a data repository*—could be created to administer the collection, access, and use of big data. The repository's mission would be to advocate for the public's interest and safeguard the public's welfare. Its functions might include:

- regulating all aspects of the data economy
- providing independent, expert advice on data policy
- acting as a steward for aggregated personal data
- ensuring the use of data in the public interest
- supporting the development of socially useful products
- equipping organizations with data, tools, and resources

There is already precedent in the United States for institutions with functions relevant to a data repository, such as the Federal Reserve that oversees the monetary system, the Consumer Financial Protection Bureau that advocates for consumer rights, and the Office of Technology Assessment that provided expert advice and represented public values on complex technical issues. A data repository could take elements from each of these institutions, while carving its own path forward.

An institution like a data repository would be a promising step toward preventing private interests from controlling the ability to build and benefit from data-driven tech. For example, instead of a company like Uber—monopolistic, mercenary, and merciless—gathering reams of data about people's mobility for its own benefit and then charging local governments for access to its insights, a repository could ensure the data is used to enhance and expand public transportation. Whereas digital capitalism incentivizes companies to innovate methods for unending extraction and exploitation, a repository could reward those who want to provide goods and services that contribute to society by allowing them to access a stock of valuable data that has been collected in fair, transparent, and accountable ways.

At this time, a data repository is just the seed of an idea. There's still a need for more detailed proposals about how to decommodify and collectivize data, but hopefully the motivations are clear.[55] Removing data from the realm of private profit strikes a damaging blow to the extractive foundations of digital capitalism. Through public ownership, the power of data can fuel more socially beneficial innovation, its value can be more equally distributed, and its potential can be more fully unlocked.

Onward

There is still a lot of work to do. While the scale of the problems at hand are large, they are not insurmountable. Consider Isaac Newton's third law: for every action, there is an equal and opposite reaction. We now know the scope of the collective reaction required. That should not be discouraging but instead energizing. It gives us cause and direction. Indeed, look around at the surprising surge of progressive politics—despite or perhaps because of a sociopolitical and environmental climate that invites defeatism—and we can see that the kinds of organization and solidarity needed are already being forged.

The three tactics outlined above—deconstructing capital, democratizing innovation, and demanding data—contribute in their own ways to the goal of seizing smartness to build a better society.

Coda

Never let a computer tell me shit!

—Del the Funky Homosapien, lyric from the song "3030"

This book will be called dystopian. It might even be accused of alarmism.

Such reactions are to be expected in a culture that teaches us to trust in technology's benevolent power. Technological advances evoke a shared sense of awe and admiration, which historian David Nye called the "American technological sublime."[1] Not only is technology equated with progress. It also becomes a thing of divine beauty.

Whether people make the pilgrimage to Silicon Valley or camp out in front of the local "cathedrals," we can see the rapturous spirit possess them during launch events by Apple or Google. Every year, there are worshippers on the edge of holy rolling as the "evangelists"—their label, not mine—praise the glory of technology, our lord and savior.

This is a normal part of our culture. Even the less devoted geeks among us have been taught to welcome technology, or at least get out of its way. Optimism or acquiescence are the only "reasonable" options we're presented with. Anything else is branded as cynicism and pessimism.

These cultural attitudes are a tough obstacle for critical accounts to overcome. Criticism provokes immediate skepticism. People are put on the defensive from the outset. But as this book has shown, there are ample reasons to be critical of what technology has been created and how it has been wielded. Criticism of the existing order—of the people, ideas, and things that shape society—cannot afford to pull its punches. It must be, to quote Karl Marx, "ruthless in that it will shrink neither from its own discoveries, nor from conflict with the powers that be."[2]

None of the seemingly dystopian things I've detailed are from a speculative future. They are all taken straight from reality. This ain't fiction; it's description. And I'm only scratching the surface of ways in which collection and control, extraction and exploitation, are intensified by smart tech. The innovative spirit of digital capitalism refines its techniques daily.

Dystopian stories cast a shadow over any argument about the "dark side" of technology.

Reporting about a scary or creepy new technology almost inevitably includes reference to authors like George Orwell (*1984*) and Aldous Huxley (*Brave New World*). They are held up as the foreboding prophets of the information age. But they are not quite the right choices. These authors didn't anticipate how, frankly, haphazard and weird the smart society can be. They predicted a kind of surveillance and domination that operates like a superefficient, hyperrational machine. In reality, what we get is something far more surreal, shitty, glitchy, gritty, venal, and violent.

If we're looking for dystopias to tell us about digital capitalism, the question is not which stories provide the most accurate predictions of how technology will develop but rather which ones capture the mood of our present and the motivations of those in power.[3] In that case, and unfortunately for us, Orwell and Huxley are not the best choices. We should instead look to the technofascism of film director Paul Verhoeven (e.g., *RoboCop* and *Starship Troopers*) and the technoparanoia of author Philip K. Dick (e.g., *Minority Report* and *Do Androids Dream of Electric Sheep?*).

Every dystopian world is also utopian for some and quotidian for others. It's about degrees and distribution of all three dimensions.

I've shown how the harms of the smart society are spread far and run deep. People who don't experience those impacts are, however, often unaware of the extraction, exploitation, and exclusion that exists all around them—and that their lifestyles rely on. If things right now seem OK or even great, then count yourself lucky. They might not always be.

Capitalism's trajectory has been on a path toward increasingly higher rates of social inequity, economic instability, and existential insecurity.[4] The digital turn in capitalism has not disrupted these trends; if anything, it has amplified and accelerated them. There is only so much room at the top; space is limited in the affluent and stable pockets of society. Meanwhile, people are being shoved or shut out from the humdrum comforts of everyday life. For many, the mundane is aspirational. It's worth quoting again the warning told to Virginia Eubanks by a woman on welfare whose life is tracked and controlled at every step: "You should pay attention to what happens to us. You're next."[5]

If the developments I have described sound distressing, then does that mean we have somehow slipped into a real-life dystopia? If so, shouldn't we try to do something about it?

There are bright spots in the darkness. For example, in the fight to determine our future, Silicon Valley—and with it, the technological sublime—is beginning to lose ground thanks to mounting backlash by the public and pushback by the workers. At last there is an emerging distrust of the boyish charm of entrepreneurs who want to engineer a better world. There is a growing recognition that we cannot rely on tech companies to have our best interests at heart. Their actions prove it would be safer to assume the opposite—if not for nefarious reasons, then out of neglect and naivety.

This book might be called dystopian, but things don't have to be that way.

Resisting, redefining, and redesigning the smart society will be difficult, but it is necessary. Thatcher's slogan that "there is no alternative" was a declaration of triumph. Silicon Valley is already hanging the "mission accomplished" banner. It's our job to show that its celebration is premature.

Notes

Chapter 1

1. Kate Quinlan, "Smart Brush Tool Now Software Integrated," *British Dental Journal* 224 (March 2018): 461.

2. David Rose, *Enchanted Objects: Innovation, Design, and the Future of Technology* (New York: Scribner, 2014), back cover.

3. Arthur C. Clarke, *Profiles of the Future: An Inquiry into the Limits of the Possible* (New York: Henry Holt and Co., 1984), 179.

4. Frost & Sullivan, "Frost & Sullivan: Global Smart Cities Market to Reach US$1.56 Trillion by 2020," 2014, accessed December 14, 2017, https://ww2.frost.com/news/press-releases/frost-sullivan-global-smart-cities-market-reach-us156-trillion-2020; Future Cities Catapult, "Smart City Strategies: A Global Review," 2017, accessed December 14, 2017, http://futurecities.catapult.org.uk/wp-content/uploads/2017/11/GRSCS-Final-Report.pdf.

5. Gartner, "Gartner Says 8.4 Billion Connected 'Things' Will Be in Use in 2017, Up 31 Percent from 2016," 2017, accessed December 14, 2017, https://www.gartner.com/newsroom/id/3598917.

6. Anna Lauren Hoffmann, Nicholas Proferes, and Michael Zimmer, "'Making the World More Open and Connected': Mark Zuckerberg and the Discursive Construction of Facebook and Its Users," *New Media and Society* 20, no. 1 (2018): 199–218.

7. Donald MacKenzie and Judy Wajcman, eds., *The Social Shaping of Technology*, 2nd ed. (Buckingham, UK: Open University Press, 1999).

8. Langdon Winner, *Autonomous Technology: Technics-Out-of-Control as a Theme in Political Thought* (Cambridge, MA: MIT Press, 1978), 323.

9. Lawrence Lessig, "Code Is Law," *Harvard Magazine*, January 1, 2000, accessed October 11, 2018, https://harvardmagazine.com/2000/01/code -is-law-html.

10. Wendy H. K. Chun, *Control and Freedom: Power and Paranoia in the Age of Fiber Optics* (Cambridge, MA: MIT Press, 2006), 66.

11. Keller Easterling, *Extrastatecraft: The Power of Infrastructure Space* (New York: Verso, 2014), 4.

12. Jathan Sadowski and Evan Selinger, "Creating a Taxonomic Tool for Technocracy and Applying It to Silicon Valley," *Technology in Society* 38 (August 2014): 161–168.

13. Martin Gilens and Benjamin I. Page, "Testing Theories of American Politics: Elites, Interest Groups, and Average Citizens," *Perspectives on Politics* 12, no. 3 (2014): 564–578.

14. Langdon Winner, *The Whale and the Reactor: A Search for Limits in an Age of High Technology* (Chicago: University of Chicago Press, 1986), 26.

15. Rhett Jones, "Roomba's Next Big Step Is Selling Maps of Your Home to the Highest Bidder," *Gizmodo*, July 25, 2017, accessed January 14, 2018, https://www.gizmodo.com.au/2017/07/roombas-next-big-step-is -selling-maps-of-your-home-to-the-highest-bidder/.

16. David Golumbia and Chris Gilliard, "There Are No Guardrails on Our Privacy Dystopia," *Motherboard*, March 10, 2018, accessed March 14, 2018, https://motherboard.vice.com/en_us/article/zmwaee/there-are-no -guardrails-on-our-privacy-dystopia.

17. "IBM Builds a Smarter Planet," IBM, accessed August 21, 2019, https://www.ibm.com/smarterplanet/us/en/.

18. Jennings Brown, "Former Facebook Exec: 'You Don't Realise It But You Are Being Programmed,'" December 11, 2017, accessed December

13, 2017, https://www.gizmodo.com.au/2017/12/former-facebook-exec-you-dont-realise-it-but-you-are-being-programmed/.

19. Clive Thompson, *Coders: The Making of a New Tribe and the Remaking of the World* (New York: Penguin Press, 2019), 341.

20. Allan Dafoe, "On Technological Determinism: A Typology, Scope Conditions, and a Mechanism," *Science, Technology, and Human Values* 40, no. 6 (2015): 1047–1076; Leo Marx, "Does Improved Technology Mean Progress?," *Technology Review* 71 (January): 33–41; Merritt Roe Smith and Leo Marx, eds., *Does Technology Drive History?: The Dilemma of Technological Determinism* (Cambridge, MA: MIT Press, 1994); Winner, *Autonomous Technology*.

21. L. M. Sacasas, "Borg Complex: A Primer," *Frailest Things*, March 1, 2013, accessed December 21, 2017, https://thefrailestthing.com/2013/03/01/borg-complex-a-primer/.

22. Meghan O'Gieblyn, "As a God Might Be: Three Visions of Technological Progress," *Boston Review*, February 9, 2016, accessed December 14, 2017, https://bostonreview.net/books-ideas/meghan-ogieblyn-god-might-be.

23. Trevor J. Pinch and Wiebe E. Bijker, "The Social Construction of Facts and Artefacts: or How the Sociology of Science and the Sociology of Technology Might Benefit Each Other," *Social Studies of Science* 14 (1984): 399–441.

24. Among many other places, Benn can be found stating the five questions in a 2001 parliamentary hearing, accessed May 1, 2016, http://www.publications.parliament.uk/pa/cm200001/cmhansrd/vo010322/debtext/10322-13.htm.

25. Joe Shaw and Mark Graham do a fantastic job applying Benn's five questions of power to the case of Google. I'm grateful to Shaw and Graham for introducing me to Benn's framework. Joe Shaw and Mark Graham, "An Informational Right to the City?: Code, Content, Control, and the Urbanization of Information," *Antipode* 49, no. 4 (2017): 907–927.

Chapter 2

1. Laura Stevens and Heather Haddon, "Big Prize in Amazon–Whole Foods Deal: Data," *Wall Street Journal,* June 20, 2017, accessed January 3, 2018, https://www.wsj.com/articles/big-prize-in-amazon-whole-foods -deal-data-1497951004.

2. Jordan Novet, "Amazon Cloud Revenue Jumps 45 Percent in Fourth Quarter," CNBC, February 1, 2018, accessed December 5, 2018, https:// www.cnbc.com/2018/02/01/aws-earnings-q4-2017.html.

3. Joseph Turow, Lee McGuigan, and Elena R. Maris, "Making Data Mining a Natural Part of Life: Physical Retailing, Customer Surveillance and the 21st Century Social Imaginary," *European Journal of Cultural Studies* 18, no. 4–5 (2015): 464–478.

4. Joseph Turow, *The Aisles Have Eyes: How Retailers Track Your Shopping, Strip Your Privacy, and Define Your Power* (New Haven, CT: Yale University Press).

5. Amazon Go, accessed January 4, 2018, https://www.amazon.com/b ?node=16008589011.

6. Nick Wingfield, "Inside Amazon Go, a Store of the Future," *New York Times*, January 21, 2018, accessed January 21, 2018, https://www.nytimes .com/2018/01/21/technology/inside-amazon-go-a-store-of-the-future .html.

7. Hollie Shaw, "How Bricks-and-Mortar Stores Are Looking More and More Like Physical Websites," *Financial Post*, March 20, 2014, accessed January 3, 2018, http://business.financialpost.com/2014/03/20/how -bricks-and-mortar-stores-are-looking-more-and-more-like-physical -websites/.

8. Stephanie Clifford and Quentin Hardy, "Attention, Shoppers: Store Is Tracking Your Cell," *New York Times*, July 14, 2013, accessed January 3, 2017, http://www.nytimes.com/2013/07/15/business/attention -shopper-stores-are-tracking-your-cell.html?pagewanted=all.

9. Chris Frey, "Revealed: How Facial Recognition Has Invaded Shops— and Your Privacy, *Guardian*, March 3, 2016, accessed January 29, 2018,

https://www.theguardian.com/cities/2016/mar/03/revealed-facial-recog
nition-software-infiltrating-cities-saks-toronto.

10. Aaron Mak, "The List of Places That Scan Your Face Is Growing,"
Slate, December 22, 2017, accessed January 29, 2018, www.slate.com/
blogs/future_tense/2017/12/22/facial_recognition_software_is_coming
_to_industries_like_fast_food_and_luxury.html.

11. Nick Wingfield, Paul Mozur, and Michael Corkery, "Retailers Race
against Amazon to Automate Stores," *New York Times*, April 1, 2018,
accessed April 2, 2018, https://www.nytimes.com/2018/04/01/tech
nology/retailer-stores-automation-amazon.html?partner=IFTTT.

12. Amazon Go, accessed January 4, 2018, https://www.amazon.com/b
?node=16008589011.

13. Suzanne Vranica and Robert McMillan, "IBM Nearing Acquisition
of Weather Co.'s Digital and Data Assets," *Wall Street Journal*, October
27, 2015, accessed January 6, 2018, https://www.wsj.com/articles/ibm
-nearing-acquisition-of-weather-co-s-digital-and-data-assets-1445984616.

14. Jennifer Valentino-DeVries, Natasha Singer, Michael H. Keller,
and Aaron Krolik, "Your Apps Know Where You Were Last Night, and
They're Not Keeping It Secret," *New York Times*, December 10, 2018,
accessed December 12, 2018, https://www.nytimes.com/interactive/
2018/12/10/business/location-data-privacy-apps.html.

15. Andrew Ng, "Artificial Intelligence Is the New Electricity," YouTube,
February 2, 2017, accessed January 21, 2018, https://www.youtube.com/
watch?time_continue=2041&v=21EiKfQYZXc.

16. Marion Fourcade and Kieran Healy, "Seeing Like a Market," *Socio-
Economic Review* 15, no. 1 (2017): 13.

17. For a report on data capital pitched at business leaders, see MIT
Technology Review Custom and Oracle, *The Rise of Data Capital* (Cambridge, MA: MIT Technology Review Custom, 2016).

18. Jathan Sadowski, "When Data Is Capital: Datafication, Accumulation, Extraction," *Big Data and Society* 6, no. 1 (2018): 1–12.

19. "The World's Most Valuable Resource Is No Longer Oil, But
Data," *Economist*, May 6, 2017, accessed October 9, 2017, https://www

.economist.com/news/leaders/2017/05/06/the-worlds-most-valuable
-resource-is-no-longer-oil-but-data.

20. Phoebe Wall Howard, "Data Could Be What Ford Sells Next as It Looks for New Revenue," *Detroit Free Press*, November 13, 2018, accessed November 22, 2018, https://www.freep.com/story/money/cars/2018/11/13/ford-motor-credit-data-new-revenue/1967077002/.

21. John Rossman, *The Amazon Way on IoT: 10 Principles for Every Leader from the World's Leading Internet of Things Strategies* (Clyde Hill, WA: Clyde Hill Publishing, 2016), 96.

22. I first mentioned these methods of valorizing data in my academic article "When Data Is Capital." This book greatly expands on the list by explaining how these methods are applied in a wide range of cases.

23. Stuart Kirk, "Artificial Intelligence Could Yet Upend the Laws of Finance," *Financial Times*, January 22, 2018, accessed January 24, 2018, https://www.ft.com/content/8c263c06-fc70-11e7-9b32-d7d59aace167.

24. Lisa Gitelman, ed., *"Raw Data" Is an Oxymoron* (Cambridge, MA: MIT Press, 2013).

25. Siemens, "Siemens Smart Data," YouTube, September 4, 2014, accessed January 8, 2018, https://www.youtube.com/watch?v=ZxoO-DvHQRw.

26. IBM, "A World Made with Data. Made with IBM," YouTube, May 27, 2014, accessed October 9, 2017, https://www.youtube.com/watch?v=QCgzrOUd_Dc.

27. MIT Technology Review Custom and Oracle, *The Rise of Data Capital*, 3.

28. Tom Wolfe, *The Bonfire of the Vanities* (New York: Farrar, Straus and Giroux, 1987).

Chapter 3

1. Gilles Deleuze, "Postscript on the Societies of Control," *October* 59 (Winter 1992): 7.

2. For a more in-depth, theoretical analysis of the smart city in terms of Deleuze and control, see Jathan Sadowski and Frank A. Pasquale, "The Spectrum of Control: A Social Theory of the Smart City," *First Monday* 20, no. 7 (2015): n.p.

3. Michel Foucault, *The History of Sexuality. Volume 1: An Introduction*, trans. Robert Hurley (New York: Vintage, 1990).

4. Michel Foucault, *The Birth of Biopolitics: Lectures at the College de France, 1978–1979*, trans. Graham Burchell (New York: Picador, 2008). Biopower and discipline are not strictly the same thing. Biopower is the application of power to govern life, both at the levels of bodies and populations. Disciplinary power works by creating certain subjectivities in people. But the two are close enough, in theory and practice, to lump them together here.

5. Foucault, *The History of Sexuality*, 139–140.

6. Patrick O'Byrne and David Holmes, "Public Health STI/HIV Surveillance: Exploring the Society of Control," *Surveillance and Society* 7, no. 1 (2009): 61.

7. Kate Crawford and Vladan Joler, "Anatomy of an AI System," accessed December 7, 2018, https://anatomyof.ai.

8. Mark Weiser, "The Computer for the Twenty-First Century," *Scientific American* 265, no. 3 (1991): 94.

9. Susan Leigh Star, "The Ethnography of Infrastructure," *American Behavioral Scientist* 43, no. 3 (1999): 377–391.

10. Gilles Deleuze and Félix Guattari, *A Thousand Plateaus: Capitalism and Schizophrenia* (Minneapolis: University of Minnesota Press, 1987).

11. Ella Morton, "Utah Has a Forest Full of Golden Clones," Slate, May 6, 2014, accessed February 14, 2018, www.slate.com/blogs/atlas _obscura/2014/05/06/pando_the_trembling_giant_is_a_forest_of_ cloned_quaking_aspens.html.

12. Donna Haraway, *Simians, Cyborgs, and Women: The Reinvention of Nature* (New York: Routledge, 1991), 161.

13. Kevin D. Haggerty and Richard V. Ericson, "The Surveillant Assemblage," *British Journal of Sociology* 51 (2000): 611.

14. O'Byrne and Holmes, "Public Health STI/HIV Surveillance," 61.

15. Jürgen Habermas, *Between Facts and Norms: Contributions to a Discourse Theory of Law and Democracy*, trans. William Rehg (Cambridge, MA: MIT Press, 1996), 306.

16. Sadowski and Pasquale, "The Spectrum of Control."

Chapter 4

1. For a sample of key works, see Jodi Dean, "Communicative Capitalism: Circulation and the Foreclosure of Politics," *Cultural Politics* 1, no. 1 (2005): 51–74; Jathan Sadowski, "When Data Is Capital: Datafication, Accumulation, Extraction," *Big Data and Society* 6, no. 1 (2018): 1–12; Joe Shaw, "Platform Real Estate: Theory and Practice of New Urban Real Estate Markets," *Antipode*, October 17, 2018, accessed June 28, 2019, https://www.tandfonline.com/doi/full/10.1080/02723638.2018.152 4653; Nick Srnicek, *Platform Capitalism* (Cambridge, UK: Polity Press, 2016); Jim Thatcher, David O'Sullivan, and Dillon Mahmoudi, "Data Colonialism through Accumulation by Dispossession: New Metaphors for Daily Data," *Environment and Planning D* 34, no. 6 (2016): 990–1006; Shoshana Zuboff, "Big Other: Surveillance Capitalism and the Prospects of an Information Civilization," *Journal of Information Technology* 30 (2015): 75–89.

2. Srnicek, *Platform Capitalism*.

3. Shoshana Zuboff, *The Age of Surveillance Capitalism: The Fight for a Human Future at the New Frontier of Power* (New York: PublicAffairs, 2019).

4. Zuboff, *The Age of Surveillance Capitalism*, vii.

5. Sandro Mezzadra and Brett Neilson, "Operations of Capital," *South Atlantic Quarterly* 114, no. 1 (2015): 1–9.

6. bell hooks, *Feminist Theory: From Margin to Center* (Boston: South End Press, 1984).

7. Simone Browne, *Dark Matters: On the Surveillance of Blackness* (Durham, NC: Duke University Press, 2015); Jessie Daniels, Karen Gregory, and Tressie McMillan Cottom, *Digital Sociologies* (Bristol, UK: Policy Press, 2016); Safiya Umoja Noble and Brendesha M. Tynes, *The Intersectional Internet: Race, Sex, Class, and Culture Online* (New York: Peter Lang Inc., 2016); Marie Hicks, *Programmed Inequality How Britain Discarded Women Technologists and Lost Its Edge in Computing* (Cambridge, MA: MIT Press, 2017); Safiya Umoja Noble, *Algorithms of Oppression: How Search Engines Reinforce Racism* (New York: NYU Press, 2018); Virginia Eubanks, *Automating Inequality: How High-Tech Tools Profile, Police, and Punish the Poor* (New York: St. Martin's Press, 2018).

8. Mar Hicks, "Hacking the Cis-tem," *IEEE Annals of the History of Computing* 41, no. 1 (2019): 30.

9. Zachary M. Loeb, "Potential, Power and Enduring Problems: Reassembling the Anarchist Critique of Technology," *Anarchist Developments in Cultural Studies* 7, no. 1–2 (2015): 103.

10. As social and biological scientists have shown, the natural/artificial divide is a distraction from meaningful questions about how we actually conceive and build our environments. See Donna Haraway, "A Cyborg Manifesto: Science, Technology, and Socialist-Feminism in the Late Twentieth Century," in *Simians, Cyborgs, and Women: The Reinvention of Nature* (New York: Routledge, 1991), 149–181; Bruno Latour, *We Have Never Been Modern*, trans. Catherine Porter (Cambridge, MA: Harvard University Press, 1989).

11. Simon Marvin and Jonathan Rutherford, "Controlled Environments: An Urban Research Agenda on Microclimatic Enclosure," *Urban Studies* 55, no. 6 (2018): 1143–1162.

12. Aimee Dirkzwager, Jimi Cornelisse, Tom Brok and Liam Corcoran, "Where Does Your Data Go? Mapping the Data Flows of Nest," Masters of Media, October 25, 2017, accessed October 16, 2018, https://mastersofmedia.hum.uva.nl/blog/2017/10/25/where-does-your-data-go-mapping-the-data-flow-of-nest/.

13. Jathan Sadowski and Roy Bendor, "Selling Smartness: Corporate Narratives and the Smart City as a Sociotechnical Imaginary," *Science,*

Technology, and Human Values 44, no. 3 (2018): 540–563; Sam Palmisano, "Building a Smarter Planet: The Time to Act Is Now," Chatham House, January 12, 2010, accessed October 3, 2018, https://www.chathamhouse .org/sites/files/chathamhouse/15656_120110palmisano.pdf.

14. Cathy O'Neil, "Amazon's Gender-Biased Algorithm Is Not Alone," Bloomberg, October 17, 2018, accessed October 19, 2018, https://www .bloomberg.com/view/articles/2018-10-16/amazon-s-gender-biased -algorithm-is-not-alone.

15. Hicks, *Programmed Inequality*; Steve Lohr, "Facial Recognition Is Accurate, if You're a White Guy," *New York Times*, February 9, 2018, accessed September 12, 2018, https://www.nytimes.com/2018/02/09/ technology/facial-recognition-race-artificial-intelligence.html.

16. Bruce Schneier, *Data and Goliath: The Hidden Battles to Collect Your Data and Control Your World* (New York: W. W. Norton and Company, 2016).

17. Sandro Mezzadra and Brett Neilson, "On the Multiple Frontiers of Extraction: Excavating Contemporary Capitalism," *Cultural Studies* 31, no. 2–3 (2017): 185–204.

18. Eyal Zamir, "Contract Law and Theory—Three Views of the Cathedral," *University of Chicago Law Review* 81 (2014): 2096.

19. Kean Birch, "Market vs. Contract? The Implications of Contractual Theories of Corporate Governance to the Analysis of Neoliberalism," *Ephemera: Theory and Politics in Organizations* 16, no. 1 (2016): 124.

20. Mark Andrejevic, "The Big Data Divide," *International Journal of Communication* 8 (2014): 1674.

21. Matthew Crain, "The Limits of Transparency: Data Brokers and Commodification," *New Media and Society* 20, no. 1 (2016): 88–104.

22. Leanne Roderick, "Discipline and Power in the Digital Age: The Case of the US Consumer Data Broker Industry," *Critical Sociology* 40, no. 5 (2014): 729–746.

23. Andrejevic, "The Big Data Divide," 1682, 1685.

24. danah boyd and Kate Crawford, "Critical Questions for Big Data: Provocations for a Cultural, Technological, and Scholarly Phenomenon," *Information, Communication and Society* 15, no. 5 (2012): 662–679.

25. Michel Foucault, *Power/Knowledge: Selected Interviews and Other Writings, 1972–1977* (New York: Vintage, 1980).

26. Geoffrey C. Bowker and Susan Leigh Star, *Sorting Things Out: Classification and Its Consequences* (Cambridge, MA: MIT Press, 2000).

27. Marion Fourcade and Kieran Healy, "Classification Situations: Life-Chances in the Neoliberal Era," *Accounting, Organizations and Society* 38 (2013): 559–572.

28. Edwin Black, *IBM and the Holocaust: The Strategic Alliance between Nazi Germany and America's Most Powerful Corporation* (Washington, DC: Dialog Press, 2012).

29. Anna Lauren Hoffmann, "Data Violence and How Bad Engineering Choices Can Damage Society," Medium, May 1, 2018, accessed April 24, 2019, https://medium.com/s/story/data-violence-and-how-bad-engineering-choices-can-damage-society-39e44150e1d4.

30. Os Keyes, "Counting the Countless," Real Life, April 8, 2019, accessed April 24, 2019, https://reallifemag.com/counting-the-countless/; Hicks, "Hacking the Cis-tem."

31. This thesis is based on an argument I originally made in the following article: Jathan Sadowski, "Landlord 2.0: Tech's New Rentier Capitalism," *OneZero*, April 4, 2019, accessed April 24, 2019, https://onezero.medium.com/landlord-2-0-techs-new-rentier-capitalism-a0bfe491b463.

32. Jeff Bezos, "Opening Keynote" (talk at the MIT Emerging Technologies conference, September 27, 2006), accessed July 16, 2018, https://techtv.mit.edu/videos/16180-opening-keynote-and-keynote-interview-with-jeff-bezos.

33. "The World's Most Valuable Resource Is No Longer Oil, But Data, *Economist*, May 6, 2017, accessed October 9, 2017, https://www.economist.com/news/leaders/21721656-data-economy-demands-new-approach-antitrust-rules-worlds-most-valuable-resource.

34. Matt Taibbi, "The Great American Bubble Machine," *Rolling Stone*, April 5, 2010, accessed January 14, 2018, https://www.rollingstone.com/ politics/news/the-great-american-bubble-machine-20100405.

35. Mara Ferreri and Romola Sanyal, "Platform Economies and Urban Planning: Airbnb and Regulated Deregulation in London," *Urban Studies* 55, no. 15 (2018): 3353–3368; Hubert Horan, "Will the Growth of Uber Increase Economic Welfare? *Transportation Law Journal* 44, no. 1 (2017): 33–105; Peter Thiel, "Competition Is for Losers," *Wall Street Journal*, September 12, 2014, accessed October 10, 2018, https://www.wsj.com/ articles/peter-thiel-competition-is-for-losers-1410535536; Frank Pasquale, "From Territorial to Functional Sovereignty: The Case of Amazon," *Law and Political Economy* (blog), December, 6, 2017, accessed October 10, 2018, https://lpeblog.org/2017/12/06/from-territorial-to-functional-sovereignty -the-case-of-amazon/.

36. Elizabeth Pollman and Jordan Barry, "Regulatory Entrepreneur-ship," *Southern California Law Review* 90, no. 3 (2017): 383.

37. Pasquale, "From Territorial to Functional Sovereignty."

38. Ian Bogost, "The Problem with Ketchup Leather," *Atlantic*, November 19, 2015, accessed January 25, 2018, http://www.theatlantic.com/ technology/archive/2015/11/burgers-arent-broken/416727/.

39. Evgeny Morozov, *To Save Everything, Click Here: The Folly of Techno-logical Solutionism* (New York: PublicAffairs, 2013).

40. Jathan Sadowski and Evan Selinger, "Creating a Taxonomic Tool for Technocracy and Applying It to Silicon Valley," *Technology in Society* 38 (August 2014): 161–168.

41. Miguel Angel Centeno, "The New Leviathan: The Dynamics and Limits of Technocracy," *Theory and Society* 22, no. 3 (1993): 307–335.

42. Aarian Marshall, "Elon Musk Reveals His Awkward Dislike of Mass Transit," WIRED, December 14, 2017, accessed October 3, 2018, https:// www.wired.com/story/elon-musk-awkward-dislike-mass-transit/; Nellie Bowles, "Mark Zuckerberg Chides Board Member over 'Deeply Upsetting' India Comments," *Guardian*, February 10, 2016, accessed October 3, 2018, https://www.theguardian.com/technology/2016/feb/10/facebook

-investor-marc-andreessen-apology-offensive-india-tweet-net-neutrality
-free-basics.

43. Nicholas Negroponte, *Being Digital* (New York: Vintage Books, 1996), 229.

44. Sadowski and Bendor, "Selling Smartness."

45. Alan-Miguel Valdez, Matthew Cook, and Stephen Potter, "Road-maps to Utopia: Tales of the Smart City," *Urban Studies* 55, no. 15 (2018): 3383–3403.

46. The phrase's origin is unclear, but it appears to be based on remarks given by Donna Haraway during a 1995 talk. David Harvey and Donna Haraway, "Nature, Politics, and Possibilities: A Debate and Discussion with David Harvey and Donna Haraway," *Environment and Planning D: Society and Space* 13 (1995): 519.

47. Alex Press, "$15 Isn't Enough to Empower Amazon's Workers," Medium, October 6, 2018, accessed October 11, 2018, https://medium.com/s/powertrip/15-isnt-enough-to-empower-amazon-s-workers-9b800472fce9.

Chapter 5

1. Michael Corkery and Jessica Silver-Greenberg, "Miss a Payment?: Good Luck Moving That Car," *New York Times*, September 24, 2014, accessed January 18, 2018, https://dealbook.nytimes.com/2014/09/24/miss-a-payment-good-luck-moving-that-car.

2. Corkery and Silver-Greenberg, "Miss a Payment?"

3. Corkery and Silver-Greenberg, "Miss a Payment?"

4. Corkery and Silver-Greenberg, "Miss a Payment?"

5. Corkery and Silver-Greenberg, "Miss a Payment?"

6. Matt Turner, "We Just Got Some Data on Auto Lending, and It's Setting Off Alarm Bells," Business Insider, September 13, 2016, accessed January 18, 2018, www.businessinsider.com/jpmorgan-gordon-smith-on-auto

-lending-2016-9//?r=AU&IR=T/#one-in-eight-loans-is-to-borrowers-with
-a-sub-620-fico-score-and-has-a-loan-to-value-ratio-of-more-than-100-2.

7. "Inc. 5000 2015: The Full List," Inc., accessed July 22, 2019, https://
www.inc.com/inc5000/list/2015.

8. Corkery and Silver-Greenberg, "Miss a Payment?"

9. Alan M. White, "Borrowing While Black: Applying Fair Lending Laws
to Risk-Based Mortgage Pricing," *South Carolina Law Review* 60, no. 3
(2009): 678–706.

10. Virginia Eubanks, *Automating Inequality: How High-Tech Tools Profile,
Police, and Punish the Poor* (New York: St. Martin's Press, 2018), 9.

11. Progressive Corporation, *Linking Driving Behavior to Automobile Acci-
dents and Insurance Rate: An Analysis of Five Billion Miles Driven* (Mayfield,
OH: Progressive Corporation, 2012), 1.

12. Jathan Sadowski and Frank A. Pasquale, "The Spectrum of Control:
A Social Theory of the Smart City," *First Monday* 20, no. 7 (2015): n.p.

13. For a good overview offering an excellent review of recent books
on self-tracking and written by an author who also has a book about
self-tracking, see Natasha Dow Schüll, "Our Metrics, Ourselves," Public
Books, January 26, 2017, accessed January 10, 2018, www.publicbooks
.org/our-metrics-ourselves/. For more in-depth treatments, see also Gina
Neff and Dawn Nafus, *Self-Tracking* (Cambridge, MA: MIT Press, 2016);
Kate Crawford, Jessa Lingel, and Tero Karppi, "Our Metrics, Ourselves:
A Hundred Years of Self-Tracking from the Weight Scale to the Wrist
Wearable Device," *European Journal of Cultural Studies* 18, no. 4–5 (2015):
479–496.

14. Matthew Crain, "The Limits of Transparency: Data Brokers and
Commodification," *New Media and Society* 20, no. 1 (2016): 88–104.

15. Federal Trade Commission, *Data Brokers: A Call for Transparency and
Accountability*, May 2014, accessed January 10, 2018, https://www.ftc.gov/
system/files/documents/reports/data-brokers-call-transparency-account
ability-report-federal-trade-commission-may-2014/140527databroker
report.pdf.

16. Olivia Solon, "Credit Firm Equifax Says 143m Americans' Social Security Numbers Exposed in Hack," *Guardian*, September 8, 2017, accessed January 13, 2018, https://www.theguardian.com/us-news/2017/sep/07/equifax-credit-breach-hack-social-security.

17. Frank Pasquale, *The Black Box Society: The Secret Algorithms That Control Money and Information* (Cambridge, MA: Harvard University Press, 2015), 147.

18. Arvind Narayanan and Vitaly Shmatikov, "Robust De-anonymization of Large Sparse Datasets" (paper presented at the IEEE Symposium on Security and Privacy, Oakland, CA, May 18–20, 2008).

19. Katie Jennings, "How Your Doctor and Insurer Will Know Your Secrets—Even If You Never Tell Them," Business Insider, July 10, 2014, accessed March 22, 2018, https://www.businessinsider.com.au/hospitals-and-health-insurers-using-data-brokers-2014-7?r=US&IR=T.

20. Astra Taylor and Jathan Sadowski, "How Companies Turn Your Facebook Activity into a Credit Score," *Nation*, June 15, 2015, accessed March 22, 2018, https://www.thenation.com/article/how-companies-turn-your-facebook-activity-credit-score/.

21. Robinson and Yu, *Knowing the Score: New Data, Underwriting, and Marketing in the Consumer Credit Marketplace* (Washington DC: Team Upturn, 2014), accessed January 10, 2018, https://www.teamupturn.org/static/files/Knowing_the_Score_Oct_2014_v1_1.pdf.

22. Casey Johnston, "Data Brokers Won't Even Tell the Government How It Uses, Sells Your Data," Ars Technica, December 22, 2013, accessed January 17, 2018, https://arstechnica.com/information-technology/2013/12/data-brokers-wont-even-tell-the-government-how-it-uses-sells-your-data/.

23. Cathy O'Neil, *Weapons of Math Destruction: How Big Data Increases Inequality and Threatens Democracy* (New York: Crown, 2016).

24. Executive Office of the President, *Big Data: Seizing Opportunities, Preserving Values* (Washington DC: White House, 2014), 53.

25. Edmund Mierzwinski and Jeffrey Chester, "Selling Consumers Not Lists: The New World of Digital Decision-Making and the Role of the Fair Credit Reporting Act," *Suffolk University Law Review* 46 (2013): 845–880.

26. Taylor and Sadowski, "How Companies Turn Your Facebook Activity into a Credit Score."

27. Edmund Mierzwinski, phone interview with the author, April 28, 2015.

28. Gibson has been saying this maxim since the early 1990s. It's not clear when he first said it, but here's a place where he repeated it: William Gibson, "The Science in Science Fiction," NPR, October 22, 2018, accessed December 9, 2018, https://www.npr.org/2018/10/22/1067220/the-science-in-science-fiction.

29. John Detrixhe, "China's Ant Financial Raised Almost as Much Money as All US and European Fintech Firms Combined," Quartz, January 30, 2019, accessed April 29, 2019, https://qz.com/1537638/ant-financial-raised-almost-as-much-money-in-2018-as-all-fintechs-in-us-and-europe/.

30. Mara Hvistendahl, "Inside China's Vast New Experiment in Social Ranking," WIRED, December 14, 2017, accessed January 21, 2018, https://www.wired.com/story/age-of-social-credit/.

31. Rachel Botsman, "Big Data Meets Big Brother as China Moves to Rate Its Citizens," WIRED, October 21, 2017, accessed January 22, 2018, https://www.wired.co.uk/article/chinese-government-social-credit-score-privacy-invasion.

32. Mark Kear, "Playing the Credit Score Game: Algorithms, 'Positive' Data and the Personification of Financial Objects," *Economy and Society* 46, no. 3–4 (2017): 346–368.

33. Hvistendahl, "Inside China's Vast New Experiment in Social Ranking."

34. "China to Bar People with Bad 'Social Credit' from Planes, Trains," Reuters, March 16, 2018, accessed March 19, 2018, https://www.reuters.com/article/us-china-credit/china-to-bar-people-with-bad-social-credit-from-planes-trains-idUSKCN1GS10S.

35. Quoted in Fan Liang, Vishnupriya Das, Nadiya Kostyuk and Muzammil M. Hussain, "Constructing a Data-Driven Society: China's Social Credit System as a State Surveillance Infrastructure," *Policy and Internet* 10 (4): 431.

36. Laing, Das, Kostyuk, and Hussain, "Constructing a Data-Driven Society."

37. Simon Denyer, "China's Plan to Organize Its Society Relies on 'Big Data' to Rate Everyone," *Washington Post*, October 22, 2016, accessed January 22, 2018, https://www.washingtonpost.com/world/asia_pacific/chinas-plan-to-organize-its-whole-society-around-big-data-a-rating-for-everyone/2016/10/20/1cd0dd9c-9516-11e6-ae9d-0030ac1899cd_story.html.

38. Department of Homeland Security, "Proposed Rule—Inadmissibility on Public Charge Grounds," dhs.gov, accessed November 25, 2018, https://www.dhs.gov/publication/proposed-rule-inadmissibility-public-charge-grounds.

39. Shazeda Ahmed, "The Messy Truth about Social Credit," Logic, April 2019, accessed April 29, 2019, https://logicmag.io/07-the-messy-truth-about-social-credit/.

40. *Modern Times*, directed by Charlie Chaplin (Hollywood, CA: United Artists, 1936).

41. The following description of working in an Amazon warehouse is based on reporting by various investigative journalists cited during the section.

42. Mac McClelland, "I Was a Warehouse Wage Slave," *Mother Jones*, December 2, 2012, accessed January 29, 2018, https://www.motherjones.com/politics/2012/02/mac-mcclelland-free-online-shipping-warehouses-labor/.

43. Spencer Soper, "Inside Amazon's Warehouse," *Morning Call*, September 18, 2011, accessed January 31, 2018, www.mcall.com/news/local/amazon/mc-allentown-amazon-complaints-20110917-story.html.

44. McClelland, "I Was a Warehouse Wage Slave."

45. Jesse LeCavalier, "Human Exclusion Zones: Logistics and New Machine Landscapes," in *Machine Landscapes: Architectures of the Post Anthropocene*, ed. Liam Young (Oxford: John Wiley and Sons, 2019), 49–55.

46. Soper, "Inside Amazon's Warehouse."

47. Adam Liptak, "Supreme Court Rules against Worker Pay for Screenings in Amazon Warehouse Case," *New York Times*, December 9, 2014, accessed February 1, 2018, https://www.nytimes.com/2014/12/10/busi ness/supreme-court-rules-against-worker-pay-for-security-screenings .html.

48. McClelland, "I Was a Warehouse Wage Slave."

49. Chris Baraniuk, "How Algorithms Run Amazon's Warehouses," BBC, August 1, 2015, accessed January 31, 2018, www.bbc.com/future/ story/20150818-how-algorithms-run-amazons-warehouses.

50. Colin Lecher, "How Amazon Automatically Tracks and Fires Warehouse Workers for 'Productivity,'" Verge, April 25, 2019, accessed May 5, 2019, https://www.theverge.com/2019/4/25/18516004/amazon-ware house-fulfillment-centers-productivity-firing-terminations.

51. Simon Head, *Mindless: Why Smarter Machines Are Making Dumber Humans* (New York: Basic Books, 2014).

52. McClelland, "I Was a Warehouse Wage Slave."

53. George Bowden, "Amazon Working Conditions Claims of 'Exploitation' Prompt Calls for Inquiry," HuffPost, December 12, 2016, accessed January 31, 2018, http://www.huffingtonpost.co.uk/entry/amazon-work ing-conditions-inquiry_uk_584e7530e4b0b7ff851d3fff; Zoe Drewett, "Undercover Amazon Warehouse Pictures Show What It's Really Like to Work for Online Retailer," Metro, November 27, 2017, accessed January 31, 2018, http://metro.co.uk/2017/11/27/amazon-warehouse-staff -taken-away-in-ambulances-during-crippling-55-hour-weeks-7110708/; "Workers at Amazon's Main Italian Hub, German Warehouses Strike on Black Friday," Reuters, November 24, 2017, accessed January 31, 2018, https://www.reuters.com/article/us-amazon-italy-strike/workers-at

-amazons-main-italian-hub-german-warehouses-strike-on-black-friday
-idUSKBN1DN1DS.

54. John Jeffay, "Amazon Criticized over High Number of Warehouse Ambulance Call Outs," *Scotsman*, November 27, 2017, accessed January 31, 2018, https://www.scotsman.com/news/amazon-criticized-over-high -number-of-warehouse-ambulance-call-outs-1-4623892.

55. Soper, "Inside Amazon's Warehouse."

56. Matt Novak, "Amazon Patents Wristband to Track Hand Movements of Warehouse Employees," Gizmodo, January 31, 2018, accessed February 1, 2018, https://gizmodo.com/amazon-patents-wristband-to-track-hand -movements-of-war-1822590549?IR=T.

57. "What Amazon Does to Wages," *Economist*, January 20, 2018, accessed January 31, 2018, https://www.economist.com/news/united-states/2173 5020-worlds-largest-online-retailer-underpaying-its-employees-what -amazon-does-wages.

58. Tana Ganevea, "Work Becomes More Like Prison," Salon, February 20, 2013, accessed February 2, 2018, https://www.salon.com/2013/02/ 19/work_becomes_more_like_prison/.

59. Jörn Boewe and Johannes Schulten, *The Long Struggle of the Amazon Employees: Laboratory of Resistance* (New York: Rosa Luxemburg Stiftung, 2017), 13.

60. Karen E. C. Levy, "The Contexts of Control: Information, Power, and Truck-Driving Work," *Information Society* 31, no. 2 (2015): 160–174.

61. Christophe Haubursin, "Automation Is Coming for Truckers. But First, They're Being Watched," Vox, November 20, 2017, accessed February 2, 2018, https://www.vox.com/videos/2017/11/20/16670266/ trucking-eld-surveillance.

62. Levy, "The Contexts of Control."

63. Haubursin, "Automation Is Coming for Truckers."

64. Jodi Kantor, "Working Anything but 9 to 5 Scheduling: Technology Leaves Low-Income Parents with Hours of Chaos," *New York Times*,

August 13, 2014, accessed February 2, 2018, http://www.nytimes.com/
interactive/2014/08/13/us/starbucks-workers-scheduling-hours.html.

65. Kantor, "Working Anything but 9 to 5 Scheduling."

66. Olivia Solon, "Big Brother Isn't Just Watching: Workplace Surveillance Can Track Your Every Move," *Guardian*, November 6, 2017,
accessed November 7, 2018, https://www.theguardian.com/world/2017/
nov/06/workplace-surveillance-big-brother-technology.

67. Maggie Astor, "Microchip Implants for Employees? One Company
Says Yes," *New York Times*, July 25, 2017, accessed February 7, 2018,
https://www.nytimes.com/2017/07/25/technology/microchips-wiscon
sin-company-employees.html.

68. Astor, "Microchip Implants for Employees?"

69. Elizabeth Anderson, *Private Government: How Employers Rule Our
Lives (and Why We Don't Talk about It)* (Princeton, NJ: Princeton University Press, 2017), 39.

70. Danielle Keats Citron and Frank Pasquale, "The Scored Society: Due
Process for Automated Predictions," *Washington Law Review* 89, no. 1
(2014): 1–33.

71. Rob Aitken, "'All Data Is Credit Data': Constituting the Unbanked,"
Competition and Change 21, no. 4 (2017): 274–300.

72. Oliver Burkeman, "Why Time Management Is Ruining Our Lives,"
Guardian, December 22, 2016, accessed February 8, 2018, https://www
.theguardian.com/technology/2016/dec/22/why-time-management
-is-ruining-our-lives.

73. Harry Braverman, *Labor and Monopoly Capital: The Degradation of
Work in the Twentieth Century* (New York: Monthly Review Press, 1974).

74. Brett Frischmann and Evan Selinger, "Robots Have Already Taken
over Our Work, but They're Made of Flesh and Bone," *Guardian*, September 25, 2017, accessed February 8, 2018, https://www.theguardian.com/
commentisfree/2017/sep/25/robots-taken-over-work-jobs-economy. See
also Brett Frischmann and Evan Selinger, *Re-Engineering Humanity* (Cambridge: Cambridge University Press, 2018).

75. Mark Andrejevic, "The Big Data Divide," *International Journal of Communication* 8 (2014): 1674.

Chapter 6

1. "There's No Place Like [a Connected] Home," McKinsey & Company, accessed June 25, 2018, https://www.mckinsey.com/spContent/connect ed_homes/index.html.

2. Leah Pickett, "The Smart Home Revolution," *Appliance Design* 63, no. 1 (2015): 16–18.

3. Brian Merchant, "Nike and Boeing Are Paying Sci-Fi Writers to Predict Their Futures," Medium, November 29, 2018, accessed December 10, 2018, https://medium.com/s/thenewnew/nike-and-boeing-are-pay ing-sci-fi-writers-to-predict-their-futures-fdc4b6165fa4?fbclid=IwAR3 nZ7uUtL_svbxw6GTqOe70fWZ4zfe8OuovsUuopeORxSgSrYL-OgyR3BM.

4. Chloe Kent, "11 Reasons 'Smart House' Is the Best Disney Channel Original Movie," Bustle, May 14, 2016, accessed February 21, 2018, https://www.bustle.com/articles/147518-11-reasons-smart-house-is-the -best-disney-channel-original-movie.

5. Ruth Schwartz Cowan, *More Work for Mother: The Ironies of Household Technology from the Open Hearth to the Microwave* (New York: Basic Books, 1985).

6. Yolande Strengers and Larissa Nicholls, "Aesthetic Pleasures and Gendered Tech-Work in the 21st-Century Smart Home," *Media International Australia* 166, no. 1 (2018): 75.

7. Philip K. Dick, *Ubik* (New York: Houghton Mifflin Harcourt Publishing Company, 1969), 24–25.

8. Fabian Brunsing, "Pay & Sit: The Private Bench," Vimeo, September 4, 2008, accessed February 21, 2018, https://vimeo.com/1665301.

9. Jathan Sadowski, "Landlord 2.0: Tech's New Rentier Capitalism," *OneZero*, April 4, 2019, accessed April 24, 2019, https://onezero.medium .com/landlord-2-0-techs-new-rentier-capitalism-a0bfe491b463.

10. Desiree Fields, "The Automated Landlord: Digital Technologies and Post-Crisis Financial Accumulation," *Environment and Planning A* (2019), accessed August 21, 2019, https://journals.sagepub.com/doi/full/10.1177/0308518X19846514.

11. Nellie Bowles, "Thermostats, Locks and Lights: Digital Tools of Domestic Abuse," *New York Times*, June 23, 2018, accessed June 25, 2018, https://www.nytimes.com/2018/06/23/technology/smart-home-devices-domestic-abuse.html.

12. "Forecast Market Size of the Global Smart Home Market from 2016 to 2022 (in Billion U.S. Dollars)," Statista, 2016, accessed February 20, 2018, https://www.statista.com/statistics/682204/global-smart-home-market-size/.

13. Kim Severson, "Kitchen of the Future: Smart and Fast but Not Much Fun," *New York Times*, October 13, 2017, accessed January 14, 2018, https://www.nytimes.com/2017/10/13/dining/smart-kitchen-future.html.

14. Bruce Sterling, *The Epic Struggle for the Internet of Things* (Moscow, Russia: Strelka Press, 2014), loc. 68.

15. Adam Davidson, "A Washing Machine That Tells the Future," *New Yorker*, October 23, 2017, accessed October 23, 2017, https://www.newyorker.com/magazine/2017/10/23/a-washing-machine-that-tells-the-future.

16. Jathan Sadowski, "When Data Is Capital: Datafication, Accumulation, Extraction," *Big Data and Society* 6, no. 1 (2018): 1–12.

17. Rhett Jones, "Roomba's Next Big Step Is Selling Maps of Your Home to the Highest Bidder," Gizmodo, July 25, 2017, accessed January 14, 2018, https://www.gizmodo.com.au/2017/07/roombas-next-big-step-is-selling-maps-of-your-home-to-the-highest-bidder/.

18. Lauren Kirchner, "Your Smart Home Knows a Lot about You," ProPublica, October 9, 2015, accessed January 16, 2018, https://www.propublica.org/article/your-smart-home-knows-a-lot-about-you.

19. Ulrich Greveler, Benjamin Justus, and Dennis Loehr, "Multimedia Content Identification through Smart Meter Power Usage Profiles"

(paper presented at the Computers, Privacy, and Data Protection conference, Brussels, Belgium, January 25, 2012).

20. Sapna Maheshwari, "How Smart TVs in Millions of U.S. Homes Track More Than What's on Tonight," *New York Times*, July 5, 2018, accessed July 6, 2018, https://www.nytimes.com/2018/07/05/business/media/tv-viewer-tracking.html.

21. Justin McGuirk, "Honeywell, I'm Home! The Internet of Things and the New Domestic Landscape," e-flux, April 2015, accessed April 29, 2015, http://www.e-flux.com/journal/honeywell-im-home-the-internet -of-things-and-the-new-domestic-landscape/.

22. This section is a greatly expanded and revised version of the section I wrote about insurance in this article: Sophia Maalsen and Jathan Sadowski, "The Smart Home on FIRE: Amplifying and Accelerating Domestic Surveillance," *Surveillance and Society* 17, no. 1–2 (2019): 118–124.

23. "The Internet of Things: Opportunity for Insurers," A.T. Kearny, 2014, accessed January 16, 2018, https://www.atkearney.com/financial-services/article?/a/the-internet-of-things-opportunity-for-insurers.

24. Andrew Boyd, "Could Your Fitbit Data Be Used to Deny You Health Insurance?," Conversation, February 17, 2017, accessed February 26, 2018, https://theconversation.com/could-your-fitbit-data-be-used-to-deny -you-health-insurance-72565.

25. Gordon Hull and Frank Pasquale, "Toward a Critical Theory of Corporate Wellness," *BioSocieties* 13, no. 1 (2018): 191.

26. Derek Kravits and Marshall Allen, "Your Medical Devices Are Not Keeping Your Health Data to Themselves," ProPublica, November 21, 2018, accessed November 26, 2018, https://www.propublica.org/article/your-medical-devices-are-not-keeping-your-health-data-to-themselves.

27. Marshall Allen, "You Snooze, You Lose: Insurers Make the Old Adage Literally True," ProPublica, November 21, 2018, accessed November 26, 2018, https://www.propublica.org/article/you-snooze-you-lose-insurers -make-the-old-adage-literally-true.

28. Quoted in Stacey Higginbotham, "Why Insurance Companies Want to Subsidize Your Smart Home," *MIT Technology Review*, October 12, 2016, accessed February 26, 2018, https://www.technologyreview.com/s/602532/why-insurance-companies-want-to-subsidize-your-smart-home/.

29. Higginbotham, "Why Insurance Companies Want to Subsidize Your Smart Home."

30. Rik Myslewski, "The Internet of Things Helps Insurance Firms Reward, Punish," *Register*, May 23, 2014, accessed January 16, 2018, https://www.theregister.co.uk/2014/05/23/the_internet_of_things _helps_insurance_firms_reward_punish/.

31. IBM Institute for Business Value, *Rethinking Insurance: How Cognitive Computing Enhances Engagement and Efficiency* (Somers, NY: IBM Corporation, 2017), accessed March 24, 2018, https://www.oxfordeconomics.com/my-oxford/projects/356658.

32. See, for example, John Rappaport, "How Private Insurers Regulate Public Police," *Harvard Law Review* 130, no. 6 (2017): 1539–1614.

33. Tom Baker and Jonathan Simon, "Embracing Risk," in *Embracing Risk: The Changing Culture of Insurance and Responsibility*, ed. Tom Baker and Jonathan Simon (Chicago: University of Chicago Press, 2002), 13.

34. Scott R. Peppet, "Unraveling Privacy: The Personal Prospectus and the Threat of a Full-Disclosure Future," *Northwestern University Law Review* 105, no. 3 (2011): 1153–1204.

35. Chapo Trap House, "Episode 190—School's Out Feat. Michael Mochaidean," SoundCloud, March 4, 2018, accessed March 5, 2018, https://soundcloud.com/chapo-trap-house/episode-190-schools-out-feat -michael-mochaidean-3418.

36. Peppet, "Unraveling Privacy."

37. Kashmir Hill and Surya Mattu, "The House That Spied on Me," Gizmodo, February 8, 2018, accessed February 20, 2018, https://www .gizmodo.com.au/2018/02/the-house-that-spied-on-me/.

38. Hill and Mattu, "The House That Spied on Me."

Chapter 7

1. Jathan Sadowski and Roy Bendor, "Selling Smartness: Corporate Narratives and the Smart City as a Sociotechnical Imaginary," *Science, Technology, and Human Values* 44, no. 3 (2018): 540–563.

2. Orit Halpern, Jesse LeCavalier, Nerea Calvillo, and Wolfgang Pietsch, "Test-Bed Urbanism," *Public Culture* 25, no. 2 (2013): 273–306.

3. Linda Poon, "Sleepy in Songdo, Korea's Smartest City," CityLab, June 22, 2018, accessed December 11, 2018, https://www.citylab.com/life/2018/06/sleepy-in-songdo-koreas-smartest-city/561374/.

4. Sadowski and Bendor, "Selling Smartness."

5. Taylor Shelton, Matthew Zook, and Alan Wiig, "The 'Actually Existing Smart City,'" *Cambridge Journal of Regions, Economy, and Society* 8, no. 1 (2014): 13–25.

6. David Amsden, "Who Runs the Streets of New Orleans?," *New York Times Magazine*, July 30, 2015, accessed June 7, 2018, https://www.nytimes.com/2015/08/02/magazine/who-runs-the-streets-of-new-orleans.html.

7. Quoted in Amsden, "Who Runs the Streets of New Orleans?"

8. Amsden, "Who Runs the Streets of New Orleans?"

9. Aidan Mosselson, "Everyday Security: Privatized Policing, Local Legitimacy and Atmospheres of Control," *Urban Geography* 40, no. 1 (2018): 16–36.

10. Amsden, "Who Runs the Streets of New Orleans?"

11. Elizabeth E. Joh, "The Undue Influence of Surveillance Companies on Policing," *New York University Law Review* 92 (2017): 101–130.

12. Ali Winston and Ingrid Burrington, "A Pioneer in Predictive Policing Is Starting a Troubling New Project," Verge, April 26, 2018, accessed June 12, 2018, https://www.theverge.com/2018/4/26/17285058/predictive-policing-predpol-pentagon-ai-racial-bias; Peter Waldman, Lizette Chapman, and Jordan Roberson, "Palantir Knows Everything about You,"

Bloomberg, April 19, 2018, accessed June 12, 2018, https://www.bloom
berg.com/features/2018-palantir-peter-thiel/.

13. Waldman, Chapman, and Roberson, "Palantir Knows Everything
about You."

14. Ali Winston, "Palantir Has Secretly Been Using New Orleans to Test
Its Predictive Policing Technology," Verge, February 27, 2018, accessed
June 12, 2018, https://www.theverge.com/2018/2/27/17054740/palantir
-predictive-policing-tool-new-orleans-nopd.

15. Winston and Burrington, "A Pioneer in Predictive Policing Is Starting a Troubling New Project."

16. Andrew G. Ferguson, *The Rise of Big Data Policing: Surveillance, Race,
and the Future of Law Enforcement* (New York: NYU Press, 2017).

17. American Civil Liberties Union, *War Comes Home* (New York: American Civil Liberties Union, 2015), accessed July 25, 2018, https://www
.aclu.org/feature/war-comes-home.

18. Stephen Graham, "The Urban 'Battlespace,'" *Theory, Culture and
Society* 26, no. 7–8 (2009): 278–288.

19. Graham, "The Urban 'Battlespace,'" 284.

20. Radley Balko, *Rise of the Warrior Cop: The Militarization of America's
Police Forces* (New York: PublicAffairs, 2013); Stephen Graham, *Cities
under Siege: The New Military Urbanism* (London: Verso, 2011).

21. Shaun Walker and Oksana Grytsenko, "Text Messages Warn
Ukraine Protesters They Are 'Participants in Mass Riot,'" *Guardian*, January 21, 2014, accessed June 13, 2018, http://www.theguardian.com/
world/2014/jan/21/ukraine-unrest-text-messages-protesters-mass-riot.

22. "Stop and Frisk Data," New York Civil Liberties Union, n.d., accessed
June 21, 2018, https://www.nyclu.org/en/stop-and-frisk-data.

23. American Civil Liberties Union, *War Comes Home.*

24. Louise Amoore, "Algorithmic War: Everyday Geographies of the
War on Terror," *Antipode* 41, no. 1 (2009): 49–69.

25. Bruce Schneier, "Mission Creep: When Everything Is Terrorism," *Atlantic*, July 16, 2013, accessed June 21, 2018, https://www.theatlantic.com/politics/archive/2013/07/mission-creep-when-everything-is-terrorism/277844/.

26. Sarah Brayne, "Big Data Surveillance: The Case of Policing," *American Sociological Review* 82, no. 5 (2017): 977.

27. Paul Mozur, "Inside China's Dystopian Dreams: A.I., Shame and Lots of Cameras," *New York Times*, July 8, 2018, accessed July 24, 2018, https://www.nytimes.com/2018/07/08/business/china-surveillance-technology.html.

28. Quoted in Brayne, "Big Data Surveillance," 989.

29. Justin Jouvenal, "The New Way Police Are Surveilling You: Calculating Your Threat 'Score,'" *Washington Post*, January 10, 2016, accessed July 23, 2018, https://www.washingtonpost.com/local/public-safety/the-new-way-police-are-surveilling-you-calculating-your-threat-score/2016/01/10/e42bccac-8e15-11e5-baf4-bdf37355da0c_story.html.

30. Intrado, "Beware Incident Intelligence," ACLU of Northern California, n.d., accessed July 23, 2018, https://www.aclunc.org/docs/201512-social_media_monitoring_softare_pra_response.pdf.

31. Julia Angwin, Jeff Larson, Surya Mattu, and Lauren Kirchner, "Machine Bias," ProPublica, May 23, 2016, accessed July 23, 2018, https://www.propublica.org/article/machine-bias-risk-assessments-in-criminal-sentencing.

32. Brayne, "Big Data Surveillance," 989.

33. Emmanuel Didier, "Globalization of Quantitative Policing: Between Management and Statactivism," *Annual Review Sociology* 44 (2018): 515–534.

34. Didier, "Globalization of Quantitative Policing," 519.

35. R. Joshua Scannell, "Broken Windows, Broken Code," Real Life, August 29, 2016, accessed July 24, 2018, realifemag.com/broken-windows-broken-code.

36. Brayne, "Big Data Surveillance," 989.

37. Maurice Chammah, "Policing the Future," Verge, February 3, 2016, accessed July 24, 2018, http://www.theverge.com/2016/2/3/10895804/st-louis-police-hunchlab-predictive-policing-marshall-project.

38. Jay Stanley, "Chicago Police 'Heat List' Renews Old Fears about Government Flagging and Tagging," ACLU Free Future, February 25, 2014, accessed July 24, 2018, https://www.aclu.org/blog/privacy-technology/chicago-police-heat-list-renews-old-fears-about-government-flagging-and?redirect=blog/chicago-police-heat-list-renews-old-fears-about-government-flagging-and-tagging.

39. Theodore M. Porter, *Trust in Numbers: The Pursuit of Objectivity in Science and Public Life* (Princeton, NJ: Princeton University Press, 1996).

40. Elizabeth E. Joh, "The New Surveillance Discretion: Automated Suspicion, Big Data, and Policing," *Harvard Law and Policy Review* 10 (2016): 15.

41. Mozur, "Inside China's Dystopian Dreams."

42. Brayne, "Big Data Surveillance," 992.

43. Rob Kitchin, *Getting Smarter about Smart Cities: Improving Data Privacy and Data Security* (Dublin, Ireland: Data Protection Unit, Department of the Taoiseach, 2016), 36.

44. John Gilliom and Torin Monahan, *SuperVision: An Introduction to the Surveillance Society* (Chicago: University of Chicago Press, 2012); Bruce Schneier, *Data and Goliath: The Hidden Battles to Collect Your Data and Control Your World* (New York: W. W. Norton and Company, 2016).

45. Torin Monahan and Priscilla M. Regan, "Zones of Opacity: Data Fusion in Post 9/11 Security Organizations," *Canadian Journal of Law and Society* 27, no. 3 (2012): 301, 302.

46. Monahan and Regan, "Zones of Opacity," 307.

47. Torin Monahan and Jill A. Fisher, "Strategies for Obtaining Access to Secretive or Guarded Organizations," *Journal of Contemporary Ethnography* 44, no. 6 (2015): 709–736.

48. Priscilla M. Regan and Torin Monahan, "Beyond Counterterrorism: Data Sharing, Privacy, and Organizational Histories of DHS Fusion Centers," *International Journal of E-Politics* 4, no. 3 (2013): 1–14; Priscilla M. Regan, Torin Monahan, and Krista Craven, "Constructing the Suspicious: Data Production, Circulation, and Interpretation by DHS Fusion Centers," *Administration and Society* 47, no. 6 (2015): 740–762.

49. Sarah Brayne, "Surveillance and System Avoidance: Criminal Justice Contact and Institutional Attachment," *American Sociological Review* 70, no. 3 (2014): 367.

50. Kurt Iveson and Sophia Maalsen, "Social Control in the Networked City: Datafied Dividuals, Disciplined Individuals and Powers of Assembly," *Environment and Planning D: Society and Space* 37, no. 2 (2018): 331–349.

51. New York Police Department, "Technology," nyc.gov, n.d., accessed July 30, 2018, https://www1.nyc.gov/site/nypd/about/about-nypd/equip ment-tech/technology.page.

52. R. Joshua Scannell, *"Electric Light: Automating the Carceral State during the Quantification of Everything"* (PhD diss., City University of New York, 2018); R. Joshua Scannell, "Both a Cyborg and a Goddess: Deep Managerial Time and Informatic Governance," in *Object-Oriented Feminism*, ed. Katherine Behar (Minneapolis: University of Minnesota Press, 2016), 256.

53. Scannell, "Both a Cyborg and a Goddess," 256.

54. Andrés Luque-Ayala and Simon Marvin, "The Maintenance of Urban Circulation: An Operational Logic of Infrastructural Control," *Environment and Planning D: Society and Space* 34, no. 2 (2016): 191–208; Alan Wiig, "Secure the City, Revitalize the Zone: Smart Urbanization in Camden, New Jersey," *Environment and Planning C: Politics and Space* 36, no. 3 (2018): 403–422.

55. Monte Reel, "Secret Cameras Record Baltimore's Every Move from Above," Bloomberg Businessweek, August 23, 2016, accessed August 1, 2018, https://www.bloomberg.com/features/2016-baltimore -secret-surveillance/.

56. Alfred Ng, "Amazon's Helping Police Build a Surveillance Network with Ring Doorbells," CNET, June 5, 2019, accessed July 26, 2019, https://www.cnet.com/features/amazons-helping-police-build-a-surveillance-network-with-ring-doorbells/.

57. Kinling Lo, "In China, These Facial-Recognition Glasses Are Helping Police to Catch Criminals," *South China Morning Post*, February 7, 2018, accessed August 1, 2018, https://www.scmp.com/news/china/society/article/2132395/chinese-police-scan-suspects-using-facial-recognition-glasses.

58. James Vincent, "Artificial Intelligence Is Going to Supercharge Surveillance," Verge, January 23, 2018, accessed August 1, 2018, https://www.theverge.com/2018/1/23/16907238/artificial-intelligence-surveillance-cameras-security.

59. Woodrow Hartzog and Evan Selinger, "Facial Recognition Is the Perfect Tool for Oppression," Medium, August 2, 2018, accessed August 9, 2018, https://medium.com/s/story/facial-recognition-is-the-perfect-tool-for-oppression-bc2a08f0fe66.

60. Colleen McCue, *Data Mining and Predictive Analysis: Intelligence Gathering and Crime Analysis* (New York: Butterworth-Heinemann, 2007), 48.

61. For a good manual about spotting this infrastructure, see Ingrid Burrington, *Networks of New York: An Illustrated Field Guide to Urban Internet Infrastructure* (New York: Melville House Publishing, 2016).

62. Human Rights Watch, *Dark Side: Secret Origins of Evidence in US Criminal Cases*, accessed August 7, 2018, https://www.hrw.org/report/2018/01/09/dark-side/secret-origins-evidence-us-criminal-cases.

63. Jenna Burrell, "How the Machine "Thinks": Understanding Opacity in Machine Learning Algorithms," *Big Data and Society* 3, no. 1 (2016): 1–12.

64. Kristian Lum and William Isaac, "To Predict and Serve?," *Significance* 13, no. 5 (2016): 14–19; Virginia Eubanks, *Automating Inequality: How High-Tech Tools Profile, Police, and Punish the Poor* (New York: St. Martin's Press, 2018); Jessica Saunders, Priscilla Hunt, and John S. Hollywood, "Predictions Put into Practice: A Quasi-Experimental Evaluation of

Chicago's Predictive Policing Pilot," *Journal of Experimental Criminology* 12, no. 3 (2016): 347–371.

65. Scannell, "Both a Cyborg and a Goddess."

66. Winston and Burrington, "A Pioneer in Predictive Policing Is Starting a Troubling New Project."

67. Michel Foucault, *The History of Sexuality. Volume 1: An Introduction*, trans. Robert Hurley (New York: Vintage, 1990), 140.

68. Invisible Committee, *To Our Friends*, trans. Robert Hurley (Cambridge, MA: MIT Press, 2015), 57.

Chapter 8

1. Jathan Sadowski, "*Selling Smartness: Visions and Politics of the Smart City*" (PhD diss., Arizona State University, 2016).

2. Langdon Winner, "Do Artifacts Have Politics?," *Daedalus* 109, no. 1 (1980): 125.

3. Quoted in Nick Srnicek and Alex Williams, *Inventing the Future: Postcapitalism and a World without Work* (London: Verso, 2015), 69.

4. Adam Barr, "Microresistance: Inside the Day of a Supermarket Picker," Notes from Below, March 30, 2018, accessed October 29, 2018, https://notesfrombelow.org/article/inside-the-day-of-a-supermarket-picker.

5. Ifeoma Ajunwa, Kate Crawford and Jason Schultz, "Limitless Worker Surveillance," *California Law Review* 105 (2017): 735–776.

6. Barr, "Microresistance."

7. Elizabeth Gurley Flynn, *Sabotage: The Conscious Withdrawal of the Workers' Industrial Efficiency* (Chicago: IWW Publishing Bureau, 1917).

8. The name comes from the supposed leader of the group, Ned Ludd, who may not have been a real person, but that doesn't matter here.

9. Robert Byrne, "A Nod to Ned Ludd," *Baffler*, August 2013, accessed October 30, 2018, https://thebaffler.com/salvos/a-nod-to-ned-ludd.

10. Byrne, "A Nod to Ned Ludd."

11. Karl Marx, *Capital, Volume 1*, trans. Ben Fowkes (London: Penguin Classics, 1990), 554–555.

12. In *Autonomous Technology*, Winner outlined what he called "Luddism as an epistemology," which is a more philosophical complement to the tactical unmaking that I describe here. Langdon Winner, *Autonomous Technology: Technics-Out-of-Control as a Theme in Political Thought* (Cambridge, MA: MIT Press, 1978).

13. Cynthia Selin and Jathan Sadowski, "Against Blank Slate Futuring: Noticing Obduracy in the City through Experiential Methods of Public Engagement," in *Remaking Participation: Science, Environment and Emergent Publics*, ed. Jason Chilvers and Matthew Kearnes (New York: Routledge, 2015), 218–237.

14. Walter Benjamin, "The Destructive Character," *Frankfurter Zeitung*, November 20, 1931, accessed December 17, 2018, https://www.revista punkto.com/2011/12/destructive-character-walter-benjamin.html.

15. Andrew Russell and Lee Vinsel, "Hail the Maintainers," Aeon Magazine, April 7, 2016, accessed July 29, 2019, https://aeon.co/essays/innovation-is-overvalued-maintenance-often-matters-more.

16. Jay Stanley, "The Virtues of Dumbness," ACLU Free Future, September 30, 2015, accessed November 19, 2018, https://www.aclu.org/blog/privacy-technology/surveillance-technologies/virtues-dumbness.

17. Marx, *Capital*, 554–555.

18. Sam Palmisano, "Building a Smarter Planet: The Time to Act Is Now," Chatham House, January 12, 2010, accessed October 3, 2018, https://www.chathamhouse.org/sites/files/chathamhouse/15656_120110palm isano.pdf.

19. Torin Monahan, "The Right to Hide? Anti-Surveillance Camouflage and the Aestheticization of Resistance," *Communication and Critical/Cultural Studies* 12, no. 2 (2015): 159–178.

20. Ronald Kline and Trevor Pinch, "Users as Agents of Technological Change: The Social Construction of the Automobile in the Rural United States," *Technology and Culture* 37, no. 4 (1996): 763–795.

21. William Gibson, *Distrust That Particular Flavor* (New York: Putnam, 2012), 10.

22. Adam Thierer, *Permissonless Innovation: The Continuing Case for Comprehensive Technological Freedom* (Arlington, VA: Mercatus Center, 2016).

23. Nancy Ettlinger, "Algorithmic Affordances for Productive Resistance," *Big Data and Society* 5, no. 1 (2018), accessed July 8, 2019, https://journals.sagepub.com/doi/10.1177/2053951718771399.

24. David H. Guston, "Innovation Policy: Not Just a Jumbo Shrimp," *Nature* 454 (2008): 940–941.

25. Michael Polanyi, "The Republic of Science: Its Political and Economic Theory," *Minerva* 1, no. 1 (1962): 62.

26. David H. Guston, "The Pumpkin or the Tiger? Michael Polanyi, Frederick Soddy, and Anticipating Emerging Technologies," *Minerva* 50, no. 3 (2012): 363–379.

27. Candida Brush, Patricia Greene, Lakshmi Balachandra, and Amy Davis, "The Gender Gap in Venture Capital—Progress, Problems, and Perspectives," *Venture Capital: An International Journal of Entrepreneurial Finance* 20, no. 2 (2018): 115–136; Sarah Myers West, Meredith Whittaker, and Kate Crawford, *Discriminating Systems: Gender, Race, and Power in AI* (New York: AI Now Institute, 2019).

28. Ray Fisman and Tim Sullivan, "The Internet of 'Stuff Your Mom Won't Do for You Anymore,'" *Harvard Business Review*, July 26, 2016, accessed November 1, 2018, https://hbr.org/2016/07/the-internet-of-stuff-your-mom-wont-do-for-you-anymore.

29. Paolo Cardullo and Rob Kitchin, "Smart Urbanism and Smart Citizenship: The Neoliberal Logic of 'Citizen-Focused' Smart Cites in Europe," *Environment and Planning C: Politics and Space*, 2018, DOI: 10.1177/0263774X18806508

30. Richard E. Sclove, *Democracy and Technology* (New York: Guilford Press, 1995), 27.

31. Wendy Brown, "Sacrificial Citizenship: Neoliberalism, Human Capital, and Austerity Politics," *Constellations* 23, no. 1 (2016): 3–14.

32. Frank Pasquale, *The Black Box Society: The Secret Algorithms That Control Money and Information* (Cambridge, MA: Harvard University Press, 2015).

33. Jathan Sadowski, "Office of Technology Assessment: History, Implementation, and Participatory Critique," *Technology in Society* 42 (2015): 9–20; Jathan Sadowski and David H. Guston, "Technology Assessment in the USA: Distributed Institutional Governance," *Technology Assessment—Theory and Practice* 24, no. 1 (2015): 53–59; Cynthia Selin, Kelly Campbell Rawlings, Kathryn de Ridder-Vignone, Jathan Sadowski, Carlo Altamirano Allende, Gretchen Gano, Sarah R. Davies, and David H. Guston, "Experiments in Engagement: Designing Public Engagement with Science and Technology for Capacity Building," *Public Understanding of Science* 26, no. 6 (2017): 634–649; Ben A. Wender, Rider W. Foley, Troy A. Hottle, Jathan Sadowski, Valentina Prodo-Lopez, Daniel A. Eisenberg, Lise Laurin, and Thomas P. Seager, "Anticipatory Life Cycle Assessment for Responsible Research and Innovation," *Journal of Responsible Innovation* 1, no. 2 (2014): 200–207.

34. Those who want a more detailed argument should start with the following two books, which elaborate on each of the two reforms I outline. For the first, see Sclove, *Democracy and Technology*. For the second, see Pasquale, *The Black Box Society*.

35. This section builds on a detailed report about the Lucas Plan written for the Social, Technological, and Environmental Pathways to Sustainability (STEPS) Centre: Adrian Smith, "Socially Useful Production," STEPS Working Paper (Brighton, UK: STEPS Centre, 2014), 1 (emphasis added).

36. Smith, "Socially Useful Production," 5.

37. Mike Cooley, *Architect or Bee? The Human Price of Technology*, 2nd ed. (London: Hogarth Press, 1987), 139.

38. Smith, "Socially Useful Production," 2.

39. Quoted in STEPS Centre, "Lucas Plan Documentary," YouTube, January 16, 1978, accessed November 8, 2018, https://www.youtube.com/watch?v=0pgQqfpub-c.

40. STEPS Centre, "Lucas Plan Documentary."

41. Mariana Mazzucato, *The Entrepreneurial State: Debunking Public vs. Private Sector Myths*, rev. ed. (New York: PublicAffairs, 2015).

42. Olivia Solon and Sabrina Siddiqui, "Forget Wall Street—Silicon Valley Is the New Political Power in Washington," *Guardian*, September 3, 2017, accessed November 20, 2018, https://www.theguardian.com/technology/2017/sep/03/silicon-valley-politics-lobbying-washington.

43. Moira Weigel, "Coders of the World, Unite: Can Silicon Valley Workers Curb the Power of Big Tech?," *Guardian*, October 31, 2017, accessed November 9, 2018, https://www.theguardian.com/news/2017/oct/31/coders-of-the-world-unite-can-silicon-valley-workers-curb-the-power-of-big-tech.

44. Federal Trade Commission, *Data Brokers: A Call for Transparency and Accountability* (Washington, DC: Federal Trade Commission, 2014).

45. Sheryl Frenkel, Nicholas Confessore, Cecilia Kang, Matthew Rosenberg, and Jack Nicas, "Delay, Deny and Deflect: How Facebook's Leaders Fought through Crisis," *New York Times*, November 14, 2018, accessed November 22, 2018, https://www.nytimes.com/2018/11/14/technology/facebook-data-russia-election-racism.html.

46. Derek Thompson, "Amazon's HQ2 Spectacle Isn't Just Shameful—It Should Be Illegal," *Atlantic*, November 12, 2018, accessed November 22, 2018, https://www.theatlantic.com/ideas/archive/2018/11/amazons-hq2-spectacle-should-be-illegal/575539; Jathan Sadowski, "Tech Companies Want to Run Our Cities," Medium, October 19, 2018, accessed November 22, 2018, https://medium.com/s/story/tech-companies-want-to-run-our-cities-d6c2482bf228.

47. Katrina Forrester, "Known Unknowns," *Harper's*, September 2018, accessed November 22, 2018, https://harpers.org/archive/2018/09/the-known-citizen-a-history-of-privacy-in-modern-america-sarah-igo-review/.

48. Jathan Sadowski, "Why Do Big Hacks Happen? Blame Big Data," *Guardian*, September 9, 2017, accessed November 22, 2018, https://

www.theguardian.com/commentisfree/2017/sep/08/why-do-big-hacks
-happen-blame-big-data.

49. Astra Taylor and Jathan Sadowski, "How Companies Turn Your Facebook Activity into a Credit Score," *Nation*, June 15, 2015, accessed March
22, 2018, https://www.thenation.com/article/how-companies-turn-your
-facebook-activity-credit-score/.

50. Lina M. Khan, "Amazon's Antitrust Paradox," *Yale Law Journal* 126,
no. 3 (2017): 710–805.

51. Virginia Eubanks, *Automating Inequality: How High-Tech Tools Profile,
Police, and Punish the Poor* (New York: St. Martin's Press, 2018).

52. Karen Gregory, "Big Data, Like Soylent Green, Is Made of People,"
Digital Labor Working Group, November 5, 2014, accessed November
22, 2018, https://digitallabor.commons.gc.cuny.edu/2014/11/05/big-data
-like-soylent-green-is-made-of-people/.

53. Tony Smith, "Red Innovation," *Jacobin* 17 (Spring 2015): 79.

54. Nick Srnicek, "We Need to Nationalise Google, Facebook and Amazon. Here's Why," *Guardian*, August 30, 2017, accessed November 22,
2018, https://www.theguardian.com/commentisfree/2017/aug/30/nation
alise-google-facebook-amazon-data-monopoly-platform-public-interest.

55. See also Ben Tarnoff, "The Data Is Ours!," *Logic* 4 (2018): 91–110.

Coda

1. David N. Nye, *American Technological Sublime* (Cambridge, MA: MIT
Press, 1996).

2. Karl Marx, "Letter from Marx to Arnold Ruge in Dresden" (1844),
marxists.org, accessed November 29, 2018, https://www.marxists.org/
archive/marx/works/1843/letters/43_09-alt.htm.

3. Author Tim Maughan keeps a running tab of the weird and terrifying
ways our reality echoes a Paul Verhoeven film. For regular reminders that
we live in a Verhoeven movie, see @timmaughan, Twitter, July 13, 2017,

accessed November 27, 2018, https://twitter.com/timmaughan/status/885385606662172681.

4. Thomas Piketty, *Capital in the Twenty-First Century* (Cambridge, MA: Harvard University Press, 2017).

5. Virginia Eubanks, *Automating Inequality: How High-Tech Tools Profile, Police, and Punish the Poor* (New York: St. Martin's Press, 2018), 9.

Index